RETIREMENT PLANNING BLUEPRINT®

CHRISTOPHER W. KNIGHT, CFP®

DISCLOSURE

Information presented is believed to be factual and up-to-date, but we do not guarantee its accuracy, and it should not be regarded as a complete analysis of the subjects discussed. All expressions of opinion reflect the judgement of the author on the date of publication and are subject to change.

All information is based on sources deemed to be reliable, but no warranty or guarantee is made as to its accuracy or completeness. Financial calculations are based on various assumptions that may never come to pass. All examples are hypothetical and are for illustrative purposes only. Charts, graphs, and references to market returns do not represent the performance achieved by Cornerstone Planning, LLC (d/b/a Cornerstone Wealth Planning) or any of its advisory clients.

Content should not be construed as personalized investment advice, nor should it be interpreted as an offer to buy or sell any securities mentioned. A professional advisor should be consulted before implementing any of the strategies presented.

Past performance may not be indicative of future results. All investment strategies have the potential for profit or loss. Different types of investments involve varying degrees of risk, and there can be no assurance that any specific investment or strategy will be suitable or profitable for an investor. In addition, there can be no assurances that an investor's portfolio will match or outperform any benchmark. Asset allocation and diversification do not assure or guarantee better performance and cannot eliminate the risk of investment losses.

The tax, legal, and estate planning information provided is general in nature. It should not be construed as legal or tax advice. Always consult an attorney or tax professional regarding your specific legal or tax situation.

Case studies are for illustrative purposes only and should not be construed as testimonials. Every investor's situation is different, and goals may not always be achieved.

DEDICATION

To my parents, thank you for showing me the value of hard work.
To my brother, thank you for being my big brother.
To my wife, thank you for always being there.
To my children, thank you for reminding me to enjoy every day.
To my clients, thank you for letting me serve you.
To my team at Cornerstone, thank you for being a part of this great journey.
Most of all, thank you God, for giving my life purpose.

CONTENTS

PREFACE

Retirement Planning Blueprint®

The first job I ever had was working with my dad on various construction jobs. To help make ends meet for our family, my dad worked odd jobs and construction projects for friends. When I was 8 years old I began working with my dad on those jobs. I was paid $3 per hour and was provided free lunch. Looking back, those were some of the most impactful times in my life. Even though it was blistering hot during the summer, I wasn't hanging out with friends by the pool, and although the work wasn't glamorous, I learned a few key life lessons:

1. Hard work is healthy.
2. Embrace the time we are given.
3. Learn what you do well and do more of it.
4. Stay away from things you don't do well.
5. Start with a plan.

The first two are the life lessons, that looking back, I learned and have realized only over time as I've grown older. Looking back to those years, the hard work in the summers giving up "play time" to work in the hot sun, has really shaped who I am today. As well, looking back those 12+ hours days in the hot sun with my dad are some of my most cherished memories together. Time was the key way my dad showed love, and looking back that's what these long days were. A lesson of hard work and his way to show me he cared. These 12+ hour days of working together were ways he showed his love towards me. I am thankful for those days.

Numbers three and four are two lessons that I think about every day now as an owner of a Wealth Management Business. I need to focus my time and energy on the things that I do well and stay away from the things that I don't do well. Truth be told, spending time constructing decks, porches, rooms, etc., taught me one key thing…I am not good at any of those things! My mind doesn't work like an engineer. I'm not very good at building things and understanding spatial recognition. Even though I spent years on job sites, I know that construction is 100% not for me! You will never find me building things or doing projects on the weekends. I prefer to stick to #4 above and work on the things that I am good at. Helping people, leading my team, devising a solid retirement plan for clients. Those are all things that I have competence and confidence in doing.

Lastly, but most importantly for where I want to take us throughout this book is that one of the key life lessons I learned is to always start with a plan. Without a plan, we would never be able to construct a deck worth walking on, a sunroom that would hold together, or a retaining wall that would hold the water back. There is simply no way around it; without proper planning, all of our hard work would be for naught.

As I have worked with hundreds of families over the past 10+ years on their retirement planning, I have seen this constant theme, that one key separating factor between those who retire with a peaceful retirement and those that do not is simply planning well from the beginning.

I have created the Retirement Planning Blueprint® that serves as a process to help clients think proactively and comprehensively for their retirement. I believe there are six key areas of planning to focus on to create your Retirement Planning Blueprint®.

These six key areas are:

1. **The Retirement Big Picture Plan** – Are you in the ballpark of your retirement planning goals?

2. **The Retirement Tax Plan** – Are you planning for one of life's largest expenses?

3. **The Retirement Income Plan** – Are you prepared to fill in your income gap?

4. **The Retirement Investment Plan** – Are you planning for your investments in light of retirement?

5. **The Retirement Risk Management Plan** – Are you planning for the unexpected with medical and long-term care needs?

6. **The Retirement Estate Plan** – Are you planning for the known unknown of death and transference of assets?

That's what the Retirement Planning Blueprint® is all about. It's about you. It's about your money. It's about your retirement. It's about identifying the best way to plan proactively and comprehensively for retirement.

One key to remember is that everyone's Blueprint is going to be different, unique to you. This book, along with our retirement workshops, and work with clients is meant to provide folks with a framework to work through to build the retirement that they desire.

1

THE RETIREMENT BIG PICTURE PLAN

Have you saved enough?

Are you in the ballpark of your retirement planning goals?

There is a common story posed with various characters that centers around the idea that they are building with the one central idea to see the big picture vs. one small individualized view. The story goes like this:

One day a traveler, walking along a lane, came across three stonecutters working in a quarry. Each was busy cutting a block of stone. Interested to find out what they were working on, he asked the first stonecutter what he was doing. "Can't you see? I am cutting a stone!" Still no wiser, the traveler turned to the second stonecutter and asked him what he was doing. "I am cutting this block of stone to make sure that its square, and its dimensions are uniform, so that it will fit exactly in its place in a wall." A bit closer to finding out what the stonecutters were working on but still unclear, the traveler turned to the third stonecutter. He seemed to be the happiest of the three and when asked what he was doing replied, "I am building a cathedral."[1]

The clear point is that mundane tasks can in themselves feel mundane, unneeded, and even a waste of time. That's how the first part of building your Retirement Planning Blueprint® can often feel. Here we are going to talk about income, expenses, assets, liabilities, goals, etc. These are the building blocks, the stones, for which your Retirement Blueprint will be built. We must carry the big picture perspective to maintain the stamina to make it through these beginning parts of the process. Identifying and understanding these facts are the most important parts of building your Retirement Planning Blueprint®.

Goals:

In the retirement classes that I teach at various local colleges, I always draw on the white board what I call your life on one page. It is a depiction of your money on the vertical axis and your life span on the horizontal axis. I always ask the class how long we should make the horizontal axis…in other words, how long do you plan to live?! It is often entertaining to hear some of the responses that I get. The lowest number I received one time was 80 years old…there was a guy in the row behind the lady that said that, that I think was in his 70's, and it seemed that he didn't appreciate such a low age for life expectancy. Then I had a lady one time tell me her mom is turning 100 the following week and she had multiple other family members reach triple digits! She will certainly need to plan for longevity.

---

[1] https://donnaharris-moregrace.com/2011/07/21/the-big-picture/

After I write the age and money, I now draw a line that crescendos around retirement age once you stop accumulating assets and begin spending them. This line continues downward until it continues past the ending age on the diagram. This depicts that most of us will pass away with excess, simply because we don't know one key number, which is when we will die! Since we don't know that, many of us will simply live much more conservatively when it comes to spending money then we probably could if we absolutely wanted to die with $0 at the end.

What do we do with the excess becomes the big question when it comes to your goal setting. The first question is certainly, will we have excess? The second question is how much excess; and thirdly is what do we do with the excess?

I believe there are only three things we can do with the excess.

Our options are that we can:
1. Increase our Life Experiences
2. Increase our Family Legacy
3. Increase our Charitable Legacy

Here is what I mean by these three choices:

Our first option is to increase our Family Experiences. Picture yourself with a solid conservative retirement plan in place. You know that there is an extremely high likelihood that you will have excess at the end of life, which simply means more money than days to enjoy them. If you knew you would have extra at the end, what are some of the things that you would like to do today with your money? Would you want to take extra trips with the kids and grandkids? Would want to travel more? What do you want to do to have fun and to enjoy? These are the life experiences that you should enjoy as a part of your Retirement Planning Blueprint®.

A second option is to increase your Family Legacy. This is planning for the excess to be used for your children or grandchildren, either at death or before. You could plan to simply live life as you want now, and then at death whatever is remaining passes to your children or grandchildren. A second way is to do giving to your family while you are still alive. Perhaps you want to provide some annual gifting to your children to see how they would handle it before you pass. Maybe you would like to give money to your grandkids by way of paying for private school or college costs. There are many ways to set up your gifting to your family during life or at death to align with your wishes for your Family Legacy planning.

Lastly, but certainly the one that is often overlooked due to the lack of clarity with someone's financial situation, is increasing Charitable Legacy. While charitable giving is fairly lackluster on a percentage basis for most folks, I believe many more would feel comfortable with giving if they had a better idea of what their excess is in terms of their overall retirement plan. From working with clients, I have found that those who understand their retirement plan, know what their excess potential is and have planned well for their goals, end up being much more confident in making Charitable giving a core part of their retirement plan. They may give more during life, and many will set up Charitable bequests at death. This can be a challenge if you do not have a firm grasp and understanding of what your excess looks like.

The key decision is to make what I call optimal decisions across all three of these areas. To review each area in light of your goals, hopes, and dreams and to put forward resources to enjoy all three to the fullest. For many this may be overweight to Life Experiences, for others this may mean more should be left for Family Legacy, and some will find that they want to use resource towards Charitable Legacy. These decisions are fully up to you and can be much easier to decide once clarity is brought to the surface by completing your Retirement Planning Blueprint®.

Big Picture Planning basics:

There are a few essentials items that you must know to build your Retirement Planning Blueprint®. This can be the most tedious part of the planning process, but it can also be the most impactful. Understanding your current situation is very important. You must spend time understanding the basic building blocks you need to know:

- What are things that you own or your assets?
- What are things that you owe or your liabilities?
- What are your income sources? Now and in retirement.
- What are your expenses? Now and in retirement, (i.e., Will you pay off a mortgage or debt prior to or in retirement).

First let's build out your personal net worth that lists out what you own and what you owe, or what are your assets and your liabilities:

Assets:
- Checking account balance

- Savings account balance
- Money Market account balance
- After-Tax Investment account balance
- Employer Sponsored Retirement account balance (401(k) / 403(b) / 457)
- Individual Retirement Account (IRA) balance
- Roth IRA account balance
- Rental Real Estate
- Cash value of Life Insurance
- Home (estimate of Fair Market Value)
- Personal property (vehicles and other valuables)

Liabilities:
- Credit card debt
- Student loans
- Auto loans
- Primary mortgage
- Home Equity Loan

Here is an example of what is a fairly common personal net worth for someone that I begin working with that is near retirement age. For illustration purposes, let's call them Jack & Jill.

They are both age 65 and are looking to retire in the next year or so.

Assets:
- Checking account balance
  o $10,000
- Savings account balance
  o $20,000

- Money Market account balance
  - o $20,000
- After-Tax Investment account balance
  - o $50,000
- Employer Sponsored Retirement account balance (401(k) / 403(b) / 457)
  - o $500,000
    - ◊ $300,000 Jack
    - ◊ $200,000 Jill
- Individual Retirement Account (IRA) balance
  - o $200,000
    - ◊ $50,000 Jack
    - ◊ $150,000 Jill
- Roth IRA account balance
  - o $0
- Rental Real Estate
  - o $0
- Home (estimate of Fair Market Value)
  - o $300,000
- Personal property (vehicles and other valuables)
  - o $30,000
    - ◊ $10,000 car
    - ◊ $20,000 truck

Liabilities:
- Home Mortgage – just made the last payment
- No other liabilities

With a personal net worth that looks like this, we would call the cash, investment account, employer sponsored retirement accounts, and IRA's their liquid assets. These are the assets that we will look to provide income in retirement from. There are certainly things in retirement that you can do with your home as a last resort, but we will look at the plan without making changes to the primary home for now.

Based on this personal net worth their liquid assets available would be $750,000. Their total net worth would be $1,130,000. The most important figure for this exercise is understanding what their total liquid assets total to be. We will now look at the income side of the picture.

Retirement Income sources:

Since they are retiring soon, we will focus on their retirement income sources, which are estimated to be the following:

Jack Social Security benefit at age 66 - $2,200

Jill Social Security benefit at age 66 - $1,800

They have no private or Government pensions available as income sources in retirement. They estimate their monthly expenses to be around $6,000 per month.

Their income coming in through a guaranteed source is $4,000 per month. Their estimate of monthly expenses is $6,000 per month. This leaves a deficit of $2,000 per month. This deficit will be referred to as The Income Gap going forward. Jack & Jill have an income gap of $2,000 per month that they must identify how to fill. We will go through various ways to effectively use the assets to meet the income gap in a bit, but for now let's get a ballpark idea if they can fund their retirement with the liquid assets that they have accumulated.

To do this, we need to learn a financial rule of thumb:

The 4% Rule[2]:

The four percent rule dates to 1994 when William Bengen researched safe withdrawal rates for portfolio withdrawals.

The research he conducted concluded that four percent withdrawal of your liquid assets with annual increases for inflation should last for at least 30 years, which is considered a normal retirement period for someone retiring in their 60's. The reason this is helpful in our exercise of looking at the big picture is that it will help us know if you are in the ballpark of having enough saved.

Do we have enough (a ballpark view)?

Jack & Jill have $750,000 of liquid assets available to meet their retirement income needs. They have guaranteed income through Social Security of $4,000 per month. This income will also continue to increase over time (albeit some years less than others). They have an expected expense need of $6,000 per month.

This leaves them with an income gap of $2,000 per month or $24,000 per year. On a percentage basis, this means that they would need to withdraw $24,000 out of their retirement assets or a 3.2% withdrawal rate. This is well in line with the four percent rule and their plan would seem to be in a pretty good place. They have saved well and appear to be set up for a solid retirement.

What if their income gap was $3,000 per month? This would be $36,000 per year and would be 4.8% of their total liquid

---

[2] http://www.investopedia.com/terms/f/four-percent-rule.asp

assets. As the percentage drifts, higher above four percent, it will continue to make the funding of the plan long-term more challenging. Keeping the percentage of withdrawal at four percent or less is ideal, and moving above four percent and especially to five or six percent can create long-term issues.

Ultimately, if your income gap is too high, which requires an unsustainable withdrawal ratio, there are only a few real options available to lower the income gap.

These would be:

1. Work longer
2. Make more
3. Spend less
4. Die sooner (not recommended!)

Most clients do not choose number four, so we are really left with just the options to delay retirement, increase income during working years (which allows more to be saved) or spend less now and/or throughout retirement.

What if you are younger?

The personal net worth figures that I used above were illustrative of someone that is retiring very soon and in their mid-60's. Certainly, if you are in your 50's or younger and are looking at those numbers, they can certainly seem quite large and discouraging. Here is what I would recommend:

- Identify your account balances as they are now.
- Use an online calculator to help figure out how much your balances will grow to over the years until retirement age.
- For instance, if you are 55 and plan to retire at 65,

here is how you can figure this out:

o Total saved in 401k or other account — $250,000

o Annual retirement savings (you and employer match) — $20,000

o Number of years to save – 10

o Annual growth rate of investment balances (be conservative) — 6%

o Total at end of 10 years — $711,000

- Your liquid assets (if this was your only account) would be estimated to be $711,000.

- You would then calculate an estimate of expenses (remove any debts, child costs, or other items that will be gone at the end of 10 years), but add inflation onto the expense figure to account for cost 10 years from now.

- Use an estimate of your Social Security figure (go to www.ssa.gov) if you do not have a copy of a Social Security projection.

- Divide your income gap over your total liquid assets and see where you land.

- If it is over 4% spend some time figuring out how to save more over the next 10 years or plan to work longer.

Divide your age by 20 rule[3]:

One other offshoot of the four percent rule is to divide your current age by twenty to establish a safe withdrawal percentage rate based on your current age. This tends to be a bit more conservative early on in retirement and will provide

---

[3]http://www.usatoday.com/story/money/columnist/powell/2016/08/11/new-retiree-with-drawal-rate-formula-4-percent/86877234/

higher withdrawal percentages if you are older. For instance, if you retire at age 65, your beginning withdrawal percentage would be 3.25%, at age 80 it would be 4%, and at age 90 it would be 4.5%.

This doesn't provide you with an exact number or annual cash flows to support the projections, but it gives you a ballpark idea if you are on the right path. Spend time identifying your personal net worth, retirement income, expenses, and income gap!

These are the fundamental building blocks to your Retirement Planning Blueprint®. Next, we will review what is the largest expense for most of us over our lives.

2

THE RETIREMENT TAX PLAN

Where it all goes.

Are you planning for one of life's largest expenses?

Taxes are the greatest expense most Americans will ever pay.
We have all sorts of taxes: we have federal income tax, state
income tax, local taxes, sales tax, real estate tax, social security
tax, Medicare tax, unemployment tax, business registration
tax, capital gain tax, corporate income tax, trust tax, estate
tax, vehicle tax, food and beverage tax, alternative minimum
tax, and potentially many other taxes!

We will focus here on income taxes and how to potentially mitigate the taxes that you pay by utilizing proper tax planning strategies. To start let's look back at history.

1913

1913 was the first year that federal income taxes were collected. The entire tax return including instructions on completing the return was only four pages. Page two had a list of income sources and on page three contains a list of deductions. Page four contained all the instructions for completing the entire tax return. Here is a link to the full tax return if you would like to see the return in full: https://www.irs.gov/pub/irs-utl/1913.pdf

During my Retirement Planning Blueprint® class I always ask the class to guess at what rate most people in 1913 paid in income taxes. Take a minute and take a guess. If you said 5%, that's a good guess, but about five times too high! That's right, the 1913 tax rate for most folks was only 1%! The wealthiest of the wealthiest would only pay 6% on their highest income amounts.

It seems the day of tax simplicity is far gone. The key to tax planning in today's complex environment is to understand what the tax code allows and doesn't allow and how to plan to mitigate paying too much tax.

Tax Cuts and Jobs Act

If you were living in a cave with no TV, social media or radio for the past few months, you may have missed that there was a significant passing of new tax laws in 2017. This new tax bill became official law with the signing of the bill by President Trump on December 22, 2017.

While the original goal of "simplifying" the tax code may not have fully occurred, there are numerous new planning opportunities for 2018 and beyond that did not exist under the old tax code. We will walk through many of the key changes and tax planning opportunities to consider under the new tax law.

Below I will lay out many of the key tax law changes that will take place under the Tax Cuts and Jobs Act:

- **Key Individual Tax Changes:**
  o Lowers the marginal tax rates
  o Retains seven tax brackets
  o Nearly doubles the standard deduction to $12,000 for a Single filer and $24,000 for Married filers

o Caps the deduction for State, Local, Sales and Property taxes in the amount of $10,000 per year (combined amounts)

o Eliminates personal exemptions

o Increases the Child Tax Credit and increases the income phase out for being eligible for the child tax credit

o Increases income phase outs of Alternative Minimum Tax exemption

o Lowers the mortgage interest deduction to only interest related to $750,000 of mortgage debt

o Repeals itemized deduction phaseouts

o Repeals miscellaneous itemized deductions that were subject to 2% floor

o Lowers Adjusted Gross Income floor for medical expense deduction to 7.50% instead of 10.00% in current tax code (only for 2018)

o 529 "College" Savings Accounts can now be used for Private Elementary and Secondary school expenses with a limit of $10,000 per student each year

- **Key Corporate Tax Changes:**
  o Top corporate tax rate for C-Corporations is lowered to 21% from 35%

  o Increases depreciation amounts for purchases of qualified property

  o 20% deduction of business profits from taxation for pass-through businesses (certain limitations apply)

- **Key Individual Tax Changes:**
  o Top rate of 40% remains in place

  o Single estates only taxed if estate value is over $11.2

million, this is doubled from 2017 level of $5.6 million

o Married couple estates only taxed if estate value is over $22.4 million, this is doubled from 2017 level of $11.2 million (certain filings need to occur at death to ensure full exemption amounts are used properly)

How does all this actually impact me?

Let's start with a review of today's tax federal tax form, the form 1040. You are likely very familiar with what a modern day tax return looks like and here is a link to a copy if you want to review while we discuss the parts of the return (https://www.irs.gov/pub/irs-pdf/f1040.pdf). We will focus on the first two pages and the key data points on the tax returns.

The 2017 Federal 1040 as of this writing in late December 2017 is not available. There were likely concerns that some of the new tax law would have been retroactive to 2017 and would require updates to the Form 1040. The 2017 Form 1040 and even the 2018 Form 1040 (even with tax law changes), will look similar to the 2016 Form 1040, so we will use it as our guide to understand a few things about tax planning. Ultimately, the goal is to better understand what our income tax is based on so that you can perform better tax planning to mitigate your tax expense as much as possible.

Income			
Attach Form(s) **W-2 here. Also** **attach Forms** **W-2G and** **1099-R if tax** **was withheld.** If you did not get a W-2, see instructions.	7	Wages, salaries, tips, etc. Attach Form(s) W-2	7
	8a	Taxable interest. Attach Schedule B if required	8a
	b	Tax-exempt interest. Do not include on line 8a	8b
	9a	Ordinary dividends. Attach Schedule B if required	9a
	b	Qualified dividends	9b
	10	Taxable refunds, credits, or offsets of state and local income taxes	10
	11	Alimony received	11
	12	Business income or (loss). Attach Schedule C or C-EZ	12
	13	Capital gain or (loss). Attach Schedule D if required. If not required, check here ▶ ☐	13
	14	Other gains or (losses). Attach Form 4797	14
	15a	IRA distributions . 15a . b Taxable amount	15b
	16a	Pensions and annuities 16a . b Taxable amount	16b
	17	Rental real estate, royalties, partnerships, S corporations, trusts, etc. Attach Schedule E	17
	18	Farm income or (loss). Attach Schedule F	18
	19	Unemployment compensation	19
	20a	Social security benefits 20a . b Taxable amount	20b
	21	Other income. List type and amount	21
	22	Combine the amounts in the far right column for lines 7 through 21. This is your **total income** ▶	22
Adjusted **Gross** **Income**	23	Educator expenses	23
	24	Certain business expenses of reservists, performing artists, and fee-basis government officials. Attach Form 2106 or 2106-EZ	24
	25	Health savings account deduction. Attach Form 8889	25
	26	Moving expenses. Attach Form 3903	26
	27	Deductible part of self-employment tax. Attach Schedule SE	27
	28	Self-employed SEP, SIMPLE, and qualified plans	28
	29	Self-employed health insurance deduction	29
	30	Penalty on early withdrawal of savings	30
	31a	Alimony paid b Recipient's SSN ▶	31a
	32	IRA deduction	32
	33	Student loan interest deduction	33
	34	Tuition and fees. Attach Form 8917	34
	35	Domestic production activities deduction. Attach Form 8903	35
	36	Add lines 23 through 35	36
	37	Subtract line 36 from line 22. This is your **adjusted gross income** ▶	37

For Disclosure, Privacy Act, and Paperwork Reduction Act Notice, see separate instructions.   Cat. No. 11320B   Form **1040** (2016)

Key tax form 1040 data points on page one:

Income:

- Income will go between lines 7 and 21 with a total of income on line 22.

- Most folks will see most of their income while working on line 7, which is for salary based wages or income that will come through directly on a W2 form.

- Lines 8 and 9 include interest and dividends which will flow from 1099-DIV and 1099-INT forms that you receive from banks, brokerage firms, investment companies, etc.

- If you are a self-employed small business owner that files their income through Schedule C of the tax return, then your income will go on line 12.

- Capital gains (or losses) created from the sale of appreciated stock will go on line 13.

- Lines 15 and 16 are very important for retirees, as this is where a good bit of income can show up.

- Line 15 is for distributions from tax-deferred

retirement accounts. This would be a distribution from an IRA or 401k.

- Line 16 is the where any pension or annuity income will come through.
- If you own rental property, that will be on line 17 of the return.
- Line 20 is the most common place for income of a retiree, as this is where Social Security benefits are listed.

Deductions:

Several "above the line" deductions (these are before the itemized deductions that are found on Schedule A of the 1040) can lower your income before it is taxed. Here is a list of a few common ones found on the bottom of page one of the form 1040.

- Line 25 will be for your Health Savings Account contribution (unless it is deducted pre-tax through your paystub).
- If you are self-employed, line 26 will be where you list half of your self-employment tax paid and receive a deduction for that.
- If you contribute to a self-employed retirement plan such as a solo 401(k), SEP-IRA or SIMPLE IRA these contributions are listed on line 28 to offset from income.
- Line 32 is the place to list your deductible IRA contribution.
- Line 33 will be the deductible line for any deductible student loan interest that is paid during the year.

At the very bottom of the front page of the Form 1040 will provide you with what your Adjusted Gross Income (AGI) is for the year. This figure is important because it can be a determining figure in whether you can do certain things like make a deductible IRA contribution or deduct student loan interest.

Moving to page two of the 1040 we will see how our actual tax owed is calculated.

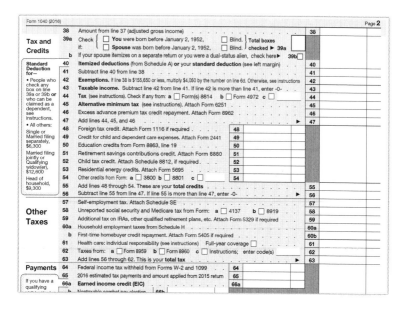

Here are the key figures on page two of the 1040:

- Itemized deductions are calculated on Schedule A of the Form 1040 and that figure OR the Standard
- Deduction carry forward to line 40. We will dive into itemized deductions in just a moment, but if your itemized deductions do not exceed the Standard Deduction that is provided, which is for tax year 2017
- $12,700 (if Married Filing Jointly), half of that amount for filing single, then you would simply use $12,700 or $6,350. This is a place of note for years

2018 and beyond. The Standard Deduction is increasing greatly to $24,000 Joint and $12,000 single. In one area of the new tax reform, this has perhaps simplified many peoples tax returns.

- Exemptions ($4,100 per person in 2017) for the taxpayer, spouse and dependents are listed on line 42. These exemptions are going away completely beginning in 2018. They have been replaced by the higher standard deduction and new rules for an increased amount of child tax credit.
- Both lines are deducted from your AGI (with one caveat that some phase outs can occur if income is above certain levels).
- This figure that is now calculated on line 43 is your Taxable Income. This is what the tax tables and your specific income tax owed is based on. This may be the most important line in the tax return, because doing whatever you can to keep this number as low as possible will cause your taxes to be mitigated.
- Line 44 will state the actual amount of Federal tax owed for the year. This figure will be offset in regard to the amount you must pay or the refund you will receive, based on the income tax withholding or estimated payments you've made during the year.
- Line 45 is the Alternative Minimum Tax (AMT) line which is an alternate calculation of your tax liability. If your Alternative Minimum Tax is higher than your regular tax liability (line 44) then you will owe the difference.
- Below line 45 will be several credits that you may be eligible for to lower tax due. These include:
  o education credits, child tax credits, residential energy credits, and others.

Progressive Tax System & Historical Tax Rates:

One other important item to note when it comes to calculating taxes is that you pay a progressive tax, where only the dollars over the threshold are paid at the higher rates. If your income is high enough to place you into the 25% bracket, you will only pay 25% tax on the income that is over the 25% tax level.

The highest tax bracket that your last dollar is taxed in is called your marginal tax rate. It doesn't mean too much other than the fact that your last dollars are taxed at that highest level.

One fun exercise I like to do in the Retirement Planning Blueprint® classes that I teach is to ask two questions when it comes to taxes.

First, I like to ask: "Do you think our current highest marginal tax rates are high, low, or an average level compared to history"?

Typically, the responses are around 10% say low, 40% — 50% say average, and 40% — 50% say high.

I then like to ask, if anyone knows what the highest marginal tax rates have been in history. I receive all kinds of responses, 50%, 60%, some say todays rates near 40%.

What's wild to know is that in the early 40's we had the highest marginal tax rate in history. It was 94%[4]!

---

[4]http://taxfoundation.org/sites/default/files/docs/fed_individual_rate_history_nominal.pdf

If you had any dollars that fell into the highest bracket, you were paying 94% of that dollar in Federal taxes.

I certainly like to pay taxes as little as anyone else does, but it sure is interesting to look at history and realize that we are paying low taxes these days compared to history.

How much tax will I owe?

The key question becomes now that you see how the tax is calculated, how much tax will you actually owe? Let's assume you are not in AMT, then you will simply take your taxable income and multiply it by the tax rates in the tax tables. The tax tables are listed below for tax year 2017 and 2018. You will see the differences in 2018 that take place. Even though the number of brackets remain the same, the marginal rates of each bracket are lower beginning in 2018.

Table 1. Single Taxable Income Tax Brackets and Rates, 2017

Rate	Taxable Income Bracket	Tax Owed
10%	$0 to $9,325	10% of Taxable Income
15%	$9,325 to $37,950	$932.50 plus 15% of the excess over $9,325
25%	$37,950 to $91,900	$5,226.25 plus 25% of the excess over $37,950
28%	$91,900 to $191,650	$18,713.75 plus 28% of the excess over $91,900
33%	$191,650 to $416,700	$46,643.75 plus 33% of the excess over $191,650
35%	$416,700 to $418,400	$120,910.25 plus 35% of the excess over $416,700
39.60%	$418,400+	$121,505.25 plus 39.6% of the excess over $418,400

Table 2. Married Filing Joint Taxable Income Tax Brackets and Rates, 2017

Rate	Taxable Income Bracket	Tax Owed
10%	$0 to $18,650	10% of taxable income
15%	$18,650 to $75,900	$1,865 plus 15% of the excess over $18,650
25%	$75,900 to $153,100	$10,452.50 plus 25% of the excess over $75,900
28%	$153,100 to $233,350	$29,752.50 plus 28% of the excess over $153,100
33%	$233,350 to $416,700	$52,222.50 plus 33% of the excess over $233,350
35%	$416,700 to $470,700	$112,728 plus 35% of the excess over $416,700
39.60%	$470,700+	$131,628 plus 39.6% of the excess over $470,700

For instance, if your taxable income was $90,000, then your first $18,650 would be paid at 10%, the next $57,250 at 15% and the last $14,100 at 25% (if Married Filing Jointly).

This can be much different than what you may think your tax is based on. For instance, if your base salary at work is $120,000, then you may think that you pay 25% tax on $120,000. When you factor in deductions and exemptions the taxable income is lowered to $90,000 and this is what you pay tax on. The example above shows how you would calculate the actual amount to be owed.

Let's see what this would look like under the new tax brackets for 2018.

Married Filing Jointly and Surviving Spouses

Taxable Income	Taxes
Up to $19,050	10% of taxable income
Over $19,050 but not over $77,400	$1,905 plus 12% of excess over $19,050
Over $77,400 but not over $165,000	$8,907 plus 22% of the excess over $77,400
Over $165,000 but not over $315,000	$28,179 plus 24% of the excess over $165,000
Over $315,000 but not over $400,000	$64,179 plus 32% of the excess over $315,000
Over $400,000 but not over $600,000	$91,379 plus 35% of the excess over $400,000
Over $600,000	$161,379 plus 37% of the excess over $600,000

Unmarried Individuals (other than Surviving Spouses and Heads of Households:

Taxable Income	Taxes
Up to $9,525	10% of taxable income
Over $9,525 but not over $38,700	$952.50 plus 12% of excess over $9,525
Over $38,700 but not over $82,500	$4,453.50 plus 22% of the excess over $38,700
Over $82,500 but not over $157,500	$14,089.50 plus 24% of the excess over $82,500
Over $157,500 but not over $200,000	$32,089.50 plus 32% of the excess over $157,500
Over $200,000 but not over $500,000	$45,689.50 plus 35% of the excess over $200,000
Over $500,000	$150,689.50 plus 37% of the excess over $500,000

In 2018, if your taxable income was $90,000, then your first $19,050 would be paid at 10%, the next $58,350 at 12% and the last $12,600 at 22% (if Married Filing Jointly).

What are all the tax form schedules?

You may wonder why all the tax form schedules that you hear about are actually important. Here is high level overview of what each schedule contains:

- Schedule A – Itemized Deductions
  - o Mortgage Interest
  - o Property taxes (up to a cap of $10,000 between combined total from property taxes and state taxes paid)
  - o State taxes paid (up to a cap of $10,000 between combined total from property taxes and state taxes paid)
  - o Charitable Giving
  - o Medical expenses (exceeding a certain threshold)
- Schedule B – Dividend and Interest
  - o Bank account interest
  - o Bond interest
  - o Dividends from after-tax investment accounts
- Schedule C – Self-employed person profit and loss
  - o Listing of all income for the business
  - o Listing of all expenses for the business
  - o Net income of income less expenses is then reported on line 12 of the tax return
- Schedule D – Capital gains
  - o Short-term capital gains are calculated based on any appreciated asset that is sold for more than the basis (what it was acquired for) and has been held for less than 12 months.
  - o Short-term capital gains are paid as ordinary income rates.

o Long-term capital gains are calculated based on any appreciated asset that is sold for more than the basis (what it was acquired for) and has been held for more than 12 months.

o Long-term capital gain rates can be as low as 0% (if a taxable income is under certain thresholds), 15% for most taxpayers, but they can be 20% for some in the highest tax brackets.

- Schedule E – Rental Income and Pass through business income

o Rental income is listed as income less expenses.

o Pass through business income such as partnerships, S-corporation distributions and LLC income are all listed on Schedule E.

These are the most common schedules and there are many others that are not as frequently used.

Taxes in Retirement:

I believe there are a few key tax data points to be aware of in retirement.

Here are the keys:

1. Understand what will show up on the return as income and what will not.

   a. Any dollars out of your tax deferred retirement accounts (IRA's, 401k's) will have that income show up right away on the tax return as income and ultimately drive up your taxable income.

   b. There are certain things that will keep your income very low. These would be living off cash instead of retirement account distributions in your early retirement years.

c. A Roth IRA will also have no tax liability created with any distributions.

2 Understand how your Social Security Benefits will be taxed. This is very important, as this is typically a good portion of a retiree's income. Here is the magic formula for figuring out how much of your Social Security Benefit is taxed.

a. You must identify your Provisional Income level.

b. Provisional Income is calculated by taking all of your income (lines 7-21, except social security income) adding in any tax-free municipal bond interest, and then adding in one half of your Social Security benefits.

c. If the total amount of those three items equal certain thresholds as outlined below, then one of three percentage levels of your Social Security Benefits will be taxed. The amount of your benefits taxed could be 0%, you could have 50% of your benefits taxed or up to 85% of your benefits may be taxed. Your benefits are all taxed as ordinary income rates, but not all your benefits are taxed.

Filing Status	Provisional Income ♦	Taxable Portion
Single	$25,000 - $34,000	Up to 50%
	over $34,000	Up to 85%
Married Filing Joint	$32,000 - $44,000	Up to 50%
	over $44,000	Up to 85%

Adjusted Gross Income (AGI)
+ Nontaxable Interest
+ 1/2 of Social Security Benefits
_____
Provisional Income ♦

How to save tax dollars:

When it comes to taxes, no one ever argues they pay too little! Let's look at some strategies to potentially mitigate your overall tax liability. Here are twenty different ways. With some I will list as basic strategies and others as more advanced. Here is a list, and I will elaborate on each idea below.

Basic tax reduction:

1. Contribute to an employer sponsored retirement plan.

2. Use a self-employed retirement program.

3. Contribute to an Individual Retirement Account (IRA).

4. Make above the line deductions.

5. Increase your itemized deductions.

6. Take advantage of tax credits.

7. Be familiar with the capital gains exclusion for sale of your primary residence.

Advanced tax planning:

1. Potentially tax-free IRA withdrawals

2. IRA to Roth IRA Conversions.

3. Running tax brackets to minimize future tax liability during Required Minimum Distributions (RMD's).

4. Capital loss harvesting.

5. Tax location of investments.

6. Net Unrealized Appreciation.

7. Gifting of Appreciated stock.

8. 0% Capital gains rates.
9. Municipal bonds.
10. Growing your health savings account.
11. Affordable care act subsidies.
12. Employing spouse and children.
13. Defined benefit plan or contribution plans for small business owners.

Here are additional details around these tax planning strategies. First, the basics, and then we will look at the details around the advanced planning strategies.

Contributing to an Employer Sponsored Retirement Plan:

One of the simplest and most convenient ways for most people to save tax dollars is by contributing to their employer sponsored retirement plans, such as 401(k)'s, 403(b)'s, 457 plans, etc. Any dollar that is invested into a pre-tax retirement plan will save a tax dollar today. One important note is that these dollars will be taxed later in life when they are withdrawn, but for now these are tax savings. This can be very impactful if you are in your peak earning years and defer money into a retirement plan. This will save tax dollars today at a potentially higher rate, then you will pay in tax later once you take the dollars out in retirement. In tax year 2016, the maximum contribution to a 401(k) is $18,000 and a catch up contribution over age 50 of $6,000 for a total maximum of $24,000.

Using a Self-Employed Retirement Plan:

The most common plans for Self-Employed people are

Self-Employed Pension's (SEP's), SIMPLE IRA's, and Solo 401k's. Each of these have various pro's and con's and maximum levels of contribution, but all can save tax dollars if contributed to during the tax year.

Contributing to an Individual Retirement Account (IRA):

IRA's are available to anyone to contribute to, although there are several rules around whether you are eligible for a deductible contribution, due to being covered by an employer sponsored plan, income thresholds, and other items, these can be good retirement savings vehicles for many people.

Above the line deductions:

These are the deductions that we reviewed at the bottom of the page on the 1040. Unlike items on Schedule A of the itemized deduction list, you do not have to reach a certain threshold (i.e., Above the standard deduction level) to have these deductions offset your income. If you have any of these items, you need to capture them on the return in the appropriate place to lower your Adjusted Gross Income.

Increase your Itemized Deductions:

As we reviewed earlier, the itemized deductions that are listed on Schedule A of the tax return will deduct from the adjusted gross income, which lowers the taxable income amount. If you are over the standard deduction then any additional itemized deductions will continue to lower the taxable income number, which will lower the overall tax bill. There are some itemized deduction limitations once you hit certain very high income levels.

Take advantage of tax credits:

Credits are a little different from deductions, in that the credit comes after the tax liability is calculated. The credits will off-set dollar for dollar the tax liability that is due.

The most common credits are for educational expenses that are paid for college courses. Most tax software and CPA's will be able to easily categorize these appropriately to ensure these are taken advantage of properly.

There is also a child tax credit that is available to most folks that have dependent children living with them. There are certain income phase outs that could limit the credits, but many will qualify for the child tax credit.

Sell your house without capital gains taxes:

Often when people retire, they want to downsize or move closer to kids and grandkids. There is always a question if they will owe taxes when they sell the home. The answer for most is no. As a married couple filing jointly you can have $500,000 of capital gains before taxes are owed on any capital gains. The one other caveat is that two out of the past five years you have used this residence as your primary residence. That would mean, if you bought a home 30 years ago, for

$150,000 and now it is worth $500,000, you would owe no capital gains on the sale. Now if you purchased the home for $150,000 and it is worth $700,000, then the $50,000 that is over the $500,000 limit would create taxable capital gains.

Details of Advanced Tax Planning Strategies:

Withdrawing dollars from an IRA without any owing any taxes:

I've found that there are a number of planning opportunities that exist when people retire, but have not obtained age 70.5 and are being forced to take money out of their retirement accounts due to Required Minimum Distributions (discussed in detail in the next chapter). Before that point retirees can better control their income that is subject to tax. By doing so properly, there are unique opportunities such as being able to withdrawal money from a retirement account tax free.

Here is an example of how this could work:

Let's suppose Jack and Jill are 65 and just retired. They are holding off on drawing Social Security benefits until age 67. They are living off of primarily non-retirement account dollars and $1,000 per month from Jack's pension. Pulling from the liquid non-retirement savings isn't creating any income for tax purposes on their 1040. The $1,000 per month pension does create $12,000 of income. Many may think they will have to pay income taxes on the $12,000 from the pension.

However, based on our earlier analysis, we now understand that our taxes owed are based on taxable income, which comes after all of our deductions or at a minimum, the standard deduction, which beginning in 2018 is $24,000 for a married couple.

Therefore, if their Adjusted Gross Income (AGI) was $12,000, their taxable income would be at a minimum reduced by the standard deduction of $24,000. Their taxable income would be AGI of $12,000 less a $24,000 standard deduction. This would make their taxable income negative $12,000. If you're wondering what the tax rate is on negative taxable income, then you've been paying attention. There isn't a tax rate on negative taxable income! For Jack and Jill they need to pull enough out of their retirement accounts (creating income) to get them back to $0 of taxable income for absolutely zero tax dollars owed. In this example they would get $12,000 out for free!

IRA to Roth IRA Conversions and running the tax brackets:

Prior to 2010, anyone with more than $100,000 Adjusted Gross Income (AGI) was not eligible to convert pre-tax IRA dollars to a Roth IRA. After 2010, the income limitations were removed and now anyone can convert pre-tax IRA dollars to a Roth IRA, regardless of income levels.

The question becomes why would you want to convert any money from an IRA to a Roth IRA, and what are the consequences of doing so?

First the key consequence to understand. Any pre-tax dollars that you convert from an IRA to a Roth IRA will go right onto line 15 as a taxable IRA distribution. You would pay ordinary income tax rates on anything that you convert.

Why would you want to convert becomes a big question?

This aligns with the idea of running the tax brackets. Here is what I mean. If you look out in the future and see that your tax rates may be higher and are unavoidable later, then you may want to take money out and pay lower taxes today, than you will in the future.

Why might you pay more in taxes later than today?

Later in this book we will go into detail on Required Minimum Distributions (RMD's), but in essence they are a minimum required amount that the IRS requires someone to take out of tax-deferred retirement accounts beginning after turning the age 70.5 (the required minimum must come out by 12/31 each year and you technically have until 4/1 after the year you turn 70.5 for the first distribution). To give you some perspective, the first distribution for most people will be around 3.65% of your IRA balance as of the end of the prior year.

For example, this is 2018 and the year you turned 70.5. The first distribution is calculated by using a factor that is created by the IRS that is the divisor. If your IRA balance on 12/31/17 was $1,000,000, the first distribution required is $1,000,000 divided by 27.4[5] (this is taken from the IRS tables) or $36,496.35.

---

[5]https://www.irs.gov/pub/irs-tege/uniform_rmd_wksht.pdf

So, if we fast forward to age 70.5 and now you are taking out $36,496 from your IRA, plus Social Security for you and your spouse, plus a pension payout, then suddenly without trying, you may be trapped in the 24%+ tax brackets forever.

IRA to Roth Conversions before RMD's begin may be worth considering if you can pay tax at a 12% bracket vs. always paying tax at the 24%+ bracket level forever into the future. This is a concept many planners refer to as running the tax brackets.

One other key benefit of a Roth IRA vs. a Traditional IRA is that unlike the Traditional IRA Required Minimum Distributions, there are no Required Minimum Distributions from Roth IRA's. Therefore, they can grow tax free throughout your lifetime.

One other IRA to Roth IRA Conversion idea:

As we've mentioned previously, there are no income limits on conversions, but there are income limits on making deductible IRA contributions. However, one tax quirk is that there are not income limits on IRA contributions that you do not take a tax deduction on. What does this mean? It means you can contribute to an IRA and not take a deduction for it, no matter what your income level is.

Now since you've put money into the IRA, but not taken a deduction for it, you can also convert the amount in the IRA to a Roth IRA and not pay tax on that conversion amount (if it hasn't grown as well!). You've created a Roth IRA contribution, even though you were over the income limits for contributing to a Roth IRA. By the way, if your income level is under around $170,000, then you can just simply contribute directly to a Roth IRA instead of jumping through these hoops. This works very well for folks that have income over these levels.

A couple caveats to this strategy:

1. If you have deductible IRA contributions already inside the IRA (or even a different IRA), then you cannot convert ONLY the non-deductible contributions. The tax-free conversion portion will be a pro-rata amount of the non-deductible contributions as a part of the total IRA amount. Only this potentially small percentage will be tax free. For example: If you had an IRA worth $100,000 and you made a non-deductible contribution this year of $5,500, and you subsequently converted $5,500 to a Roth IRA, then the tax-free portion that was converted would only be 5.5% (the $5,500 over $100,000) or $302.50 tax free. The remaining $5,197.50 would all be included as a taxable distribution on line 15 of your form 1040.

2. If you can get past #1 and have no amount except the non-deductible contribution in your IRA, then the second caveat is to understand that any earnings earned on that $5,500 (or whatever amount you contributed) will be subject to tax if it has earnings attached to it. For example: If you put $5,500 into an IRA as a non-deductible contribution, you forget to convert it to a Roth IRA and it grows for 12 months and is now worth $6,000, the $500 in gains would be subject to ordinary income tax.

If you can work through these two caveats, then it could be a very worthwhile strategy long-term to position dollars into a Roth IRA this way (again if you are over the income limits to make contributions directly).

Capital loss harvesting:

If you have after-tax investments that have a loss on paper (it is worth less than you paid for it) then you can sell that investment. The difference between what you paid for it and the what you sell it for can be used as a capital loss. The capital losses can directly offset any capital gains. If you still have losses leftover after offsetting capital gains, you can offset up to $3,000 in ordinary income.. Any capital losses remaining will carry forward indefinitely to offset gains or ordinary income in the future.

Tax location investing strategy:

If you have various buckets of money that are split between after-tax investment accounts, tax deferred accounts, and even Roth or tax-free accounts, it could make sense to position various asset classes into different buckets based on tax treatment. For instance, if bonds produce interest that is taxed at ordinary income rates, it could make sense to position more of the bonds into tax-deferred savings vehicles such as IRA's, 401k's, etc. Since capital gains and qualified dividends are taxed at lower rates than ordinary income rates, then you may want to position stocks into after-tax accounts that would produce dividends and capital gains that would be taxable at these preferential rates. If you have the third bucket, which is tax-free growth, you may want to put the highest risk/reward asset classes like small cap and emerging markets into this bucket, because they have the highest historical odds of significant appreciation.

Net Unrealized Appreciation (NUA):

NUA is a quirky tax planning strategy that only affects someone that works for a company that offers publicly traded company stock as an investment option in their 401k plan. If someone has purchased company stock over the years in their 401k, they can make a special NUA election of tax treatment after they retire and decide to transfer their 401k. The special election allows for ordinary income tax to be paid on the basis of the stock, while only owing capital gains taxes at a future time when the investments are sold out of their investment account. This can be complicated, and I highly recommend working with someone that can ensure you have made the proper elections before moving forward with this planning option.

Gifting of appreciated assets:

If you give to Church, charity, or other non-profit organizations and you have appreciated assets (stock, real estate, etc.), you may want to explore the use of appreciated property for your gift instead of giving cash. By using appreciated assets, you can avoid the capital gains if you were to sell the stock and give the cash, as well you can receive a full tax deduction of the fair market value of the stock, real estate, etc., (if it has been held for at least 12 months).

For example: If you own Apple stock that you purchased two years ago and you put $1,000 into it. Now it is worth $1,500. If you wanted to make a gift somewhere for $1,500 you could sell your stock and give the cash to charity. You will be stuck paying the capital gains tax on the $500, but you will still get a $1,500 deduction for the contribution. Alternatively, you could gift the $1,500 position of Apple stock directly to the charity. They would then sell the stock position and owe no tax since they are a non-profit. You would still get the $1,500 deduction and the charity would still have a $1,500 gift.

0% Capital Gains rates:

Based on current tax law, if you are in the 15% tax bracket or lower, your long-term capital gains rate is 0%. If your taxable income is low enough to keep you in the 15% bracket thenif you sell stock at a gain that you've held for more than one year, you would pay 0% on the capital gains (as long as the gains did not push you outside the 15% bracket).

This strategy can be very effective for people that have low basis stock, have retired, but have very low income. Selling the stock and realizing capital gains can be done in a 0% tax world if planned correctly. This can help diversify the investments without having adverse tax consequences by doing so.

Municipal Bonds:

Municipal bonds can be a great option for tax payers in the highest tax brackets. The interest received from municipal bonds are not Federally taxed, and they may not be taxed on the state level either if you use municipals from the state that you reside in.

One issue for municipal bond interest is that the interest is an add-back item for the calculation of Alternative Minimum Tax and is also used to calculate the Provisional income, which is used to calculate how much of your social security benefit will be taxed.

Growing your Health Savings Account:

Many are familiar with a Health Savings Account and being able to contribute to it as long as you have a High Deductible Health Plan. One way the Health Savings Account can also be used is to grow the funds for retiree healthcare expenses. In the meantime, the medical bills can be paid by out of pocket sources. Funds put into the Health Savings Account are provided a triple tax free benefit in that they are tax free dollars going into the account, the funds in the account grow tax free, and as long as they are used for qualified medical expenses in retirement, they can be withdrawn from the account at a future time tax free as well. The Health Savings Account can also be grown by investing the funds through various investment companies that offer this as an option.

Affordable Care Act Subsidies:

One of the biggest questions of retirees prior to being eligible for Medicare at the age of 65 is how to access health care coverage. There is certainly COBRA that will cover you for 18 months after separation from employment. Affordable Care Act policies is an option at this time as well. There are pro's and con's, but one quirk is how the subsidies for policies are calculated. This would mean that someone that is retired before Medicare age can potentially manage their income in a way that would allow for them to receive subsidies for Affordable Care Act policies. If they manage their income to not withdraw from sources that would put income directly onto their tax return (i.e., IRA or 401k withdrawals), and instead withdraw from after-tax investment accounts or cash savings, their income could be low enough to qualify for subsidies.

Employing spouse and children in a family business:

If you own a business you could look at employing your spouse and/or children. Certainly they need to perform services that would justify compensation, but by doing so there would be a number of potential positives. For the spouse, if there is a lower or no earnings history, this would allow them to establish an earnings history for Social Security benefit purposes. This could make for a substantial increase over what a spousal only benefit would amount to.

By employing children, they can have earned income that would allow for them to make contributions to a retirement vehicle such as a Roth IRA. By contributing so early, the compound interest effect of something like this could be substantial.

Defined Benefit Plan for Small Business Owners:

If you are in your peak earning years before retirement as a small business owner, you may want to investigate the use of a Defined Benefit plan for your small business. If structured properly you may be able to put away over $200,000 per year with little extra dollars required to be given to other employees (dependent on age, compensation, and length of service of other employees). These are typically ideal for a small business owner that has very high income and desires additional savings vehicles.

Other Tax Planning:

Keeping taxes at bay when changing companies:

When you leave a company, you have various options of what to do with your 401k. Typically, you can:

1. Leave it as it is (there may be a minimum balance requirement).

2. Roll it over to an Individual Retirement Account (IRA).

3. Take it out in a lump sum.

Which is best, is certainly a unique decision. Here are some details on each option below:

Option #1 Leave it as it is – One option is to leave it where it is at in the 401k at the company. This may not be a bad default option. You will still be able to invest in the options that you have invested in previously and will be familiar with the setup of the account.

A few issues that could exist with this option are:

1. **Limited investment options** – Many 401k plans have improved their investment options over the last few years, but with a 401k you are going to be limited to the options in your plan.

2. **Mandatory tax withholding on any future distributions** – When taking a distribution from your 401k, the IRS requires a 20% withholding from any 401k distributions. As well, some states have a mandatory tax withholding. If you recall as we've reviewed taxes in the past, one issue for a retiree is that

you may be in a low tax situation... much lower than the 20% required. This would mean that with every dollar you take out, you are having to take out extra to account for the 20% withholding and loaning those dollars to the Government until you file your taxes and get a refund by the following April 15.

3. **Fees can be higher (especially in smaller plans)** – Typically, the smaller the company, which means the smaller the plan, the higher the fees are likely to be. As costs for investment products like mutual funds and Exchange Traded Funds (ETF's) have continued to lower over the past number of years, this has created a potential difference in the investments you could access personally vs. through your 401k.

Option #2 Rollover to an Individual Retirement Account (IRA) - This option provides you the most flexibility from an investment and withdrawal standpoint. You can self-direct this account or work with a Financial Planner to assist in the ongoing management of the account.

Option #3: Take the funds in a Lump Sum - This option is likely not to make sense in most situations. You would be subject to paying income taxes on the entire distribution form a pre-tax retirement account. Also, if you are under age 59.5 a 10% early withdrawal penalty would be required. This create a significant tax bill for most people.

Putting it all together:

You've probably seen more on tax planning than perhaps you've ever wanted to. At the core of tax planning is simply understanding how various elements of the tax code work, what creates income, what your tax rate is based on, understanding how to save taxes, and building your plan to appropriately mitigate taxes as much as possible.

3

THE RETIREMENT INCOME PLAN

Are you prepared to fill in your income gap?

For most retirees, the main question in retirement is centered around: how will I meet my income needs in retirement? If we think back to what we did in Chapter One with the big picture view of retirement, one of the keys is to assess and determine what your Income Gap is going to be. The income gap is simply your defined income sources less your expenses. If your social security benefit is $2,000 and your spouse's is $1,500, you have no pensions and your expenses are expected to be $4,500 per month, then you have a monthly income gap of $1,000 per month. You have defined income sources which can be Social Security or private or Government defined benefit pensions. These will provide you with an ongoing monthly income stream. Let's get right to the core of most people's retirement income plan, which is Social Security benefits.

Social Security:

Everyone is familiar with Social Security. Some fear what the future may hold, others embrace the present as this benefit is a core part of their retirement income plan. Let's start with a little bit of history of Social Security, and then we will dive into the key terms and potential planning opportunities.

History of Social Security:

The Social Security Act was signed into law by President Roosevelt on August 14, 1935. As the effects of the Great Depression continued, the Federal Government created Social Security to provide a lifetime payment benefit to those who had reached age 65. One very interesting fact is in regard to the life expectancy in the 1930's. Those who were born in 1930 would have a life expectancy of 58 for males and 62 for females[6]. Although many would argue that the life expectancy was much higher for those that attained age 65, since infancy births are included in the normal life expectancy calculation, and that can skew the life expectancy estimate much lower. Regardless, either way the benefits that were projected to be

---

[6]https://www.ssa.gov/history/lifeexpect.html

paid out for a retiree in the 1930's was much less than Social Security benefits are projected to pay out to people reaching retirement age today. Current longevity for people reaching retirement age today is one of the key drivers to future funding issues.

Funding of Social Security:

It is important to understand how Social Security benefits are funded. There are three key drivers to the funding of Social Security benefits. They are payroll taxes, interest on the Social Security trust fund, and taxes on Social Security benefits.

Payroll taxes, taxes on Social Security benefits and interest on the trust fund:

Payroll tax funding is the means that is most familiar for everyone. This is the 6.2% of wages (up to a maximum, currently in 2018 of $128,400) that an employee pays and the 6.2% of wages that an employer pays on the employee wages. Together on income up to $128,400 (in 2018) there is 12.4% being paid into Social Security.

As we reviewed in the tax planning section, there is a chance that 50% or 85% of your Social Security benefits may be subject to taxation. This hasn't always been the case. In 1983, a bill was passed that allowed for retirees receiving Social Security benefits and having income over a certain level would have 50% of their benefits subject to tax. In 1994 President Clinton signed into law a bill that increased this level to 100% of benefits being taxed for the highest income retirees. These two new levels of tax created significant increases in revenue for Social Security.

Some may find this hard to believe, but from 1983 to 2009 due to the taxation of Social Security benefits there was a surplus created that built up the Social Security Trust fund. This is the Trust fund that everyone hears about being insolvent in around 20 years. We will address those concerns in just a moment.

With the Social Security trust fund, the remaining surplus is invested in Government bonds that produce a guaranteed rate of return on the trust fund. This interest allows the fund to continue to grow and be another revenue source.

These three revenue sources are the funding sources for Social Security benefits. Let's now look at some of the future funding concerns.

Future funding concerns of Social Security:

Most people have heard about the funding issues that are projected for Social Security benefits. The trust fund that covers the gap between the benefits being paid and the revenue being received from the other sources is projected to be exhausted by 2035. This is nothing to take lightly, but it is helpful to understand that it doesn't mean all benefits are going to completely go away even if the trust fund was insolvent. Even without the trust fund, the projections from Social Security[7] indicate that around 75% of scheduled benefits would still be met by way of the other funding sources. Again, this is if nothing at all is done to combat the potential funding issues.

---

[7] https://www.ssa.gov/policy/docs/ssb/v70n3/v70n3p111.html

What can be done to help the funding issues?

There are a few levers that can be pulled to increase the funding and longevity of Social Security. Here are a few options:

- Increase the retirement age gradually from the current Full Retirement Age (FRA) maximum of 67 to something higher such as 69 or 70.
- Increase the payroll tax level from 6.2% to something higher.
- Increase the level of income that is subject to payroll taxes.
- Increase the taxation on benefits from only 50% or 85% to something higher.
- Decrease the Cost of Living Allowances (COLA) for retirees receiving benefits.

Everyone will certainly have various opinions on which option is best. The most logical option would be to use multiple levers so that one group of retirees or younger folks still paying into Social Security aren't overly affected.

How to find information on your benefits projections:

I recommend setting up an account on www.SSA.gov. This is a great site that will list all your projected benefits, earnings history, etc. This is important to have access to now that the Social Security Administration doesn't send out annual benefit statements.

Key Social Security items to know:

Your benefit projection is based on the top 35 years of earnings history. This top 35 years creates what is known as your Averaged Indexed Monthly Earnings (AIME). Past years of earnings are indexed to equate to current years' dollars and averaged over those 35 years.

To be eligible for retiree benefits you must have 40 quarters of earnings (subject to a minimum amount of earnings in a quarter, in 2016 it is $1,300).

A retiree's benefit is based on their Full Retirement Age (FRA) benefit, known as the Primary Insurance Amount (PIA).

A spouse of an eligible retiree is automatically eligible for spousal Social Security benefits. The spousal benefit is equal to 50% of the retiree benefits, Full Retirement Age benefit, if the spouse has obtained their FRA.

A retiree can take a reduced benefit as early as age 62, although the benefit is reduced by approximately 6% a year for every year that it is taken early[8].

A retiree can receive a larger benefit by accruing delayed retirement credits if taking Social Security benefits is delayed. This deferral can continue with annual increases of about 8% per year[9]. There are no additional benefits after obtaining age 70.

---

[8] https://www.ssa.gov/oact/quickcalc/earlyretire.html
[9] https://www.ssa.gov/planners/retire/1943-delay.html

For a spousal benefit, the max spousal benefit is 50% of the PIA of the spousal retiree. The spousal benefit does not increase beyond the 50% of PIA level. It wouldn't make sense for a spouse to delay taking the benefit beyond their own FRA. One other quirk in taking spousal benefits is to understand that spousal benefits are allowed payable once the retiree that they are based on is receiving benefits.

If you take benefits before your FRA, then you are subject to an earnings test that will require a payback of some benefits that are received. In 2018, the earnings test is $17,040. If you earn over $17,040 and you are under FRA, you will have to pay back $1 for every $2 that you receive over the $17,040 level. For example, if you earn $30,000, then you have earned $12,960 too much and will pay back 50% of that overage or $6,480. This earnings test is only in effect until you reach FRA.

Full Retirement Age (FRA):

We've spent a lot of time talking about a retiree's FRA. Here is a chart that outlines the FRA defined by the year that you were born. This is the age in which you can receive your PIA and have no earnings test that may reduce your benefits.

Full Retirement Ages	
If you were born in:	Your full retirement age is:
1943-1954	66
1955	66 and 2 months
1956	66 and 4 months
1957	66 and 6 months
1958	66 and 8 months
1959	66 and 10 months
1960 or later	67

A note on a few other Social Security benefits:

Survivor benefit:

A widow or widower is eligible for the deceased spouse's retirement benefit if it higher than their own benefit. This benefit can be taken as early as age 60. Although it will be reduced if taken before FRA of the survivor.

Divorced spouse benefits:

As long as you were married for 10 years and have not remarried, you are eligible for a spousal benefit on your ex-spouse's earnings history. Unlike the spousal benefit your ex-spouse does not have to be receiving benefits for you to be able to begin receiving spousal benefits. As long as you are age 62 and haven't remarried you are eligible for divorced benefits.

Social Security coordination:

The question becomes how to plan properly and coordinate benefits between spouses. There are several key decisions and questions to think through:

1. If longevity runs in your family, and do you prefer to plan conservatively? If so, you may want to plan on delaying Social Security benefits as long as possible so that you have maximum benefits for a longer period of time.

2. If you have poor health and potentially a shorter life expectancy? If so, you may want to plan on taking benefits earlier.

3. If one spouse is a significantly higher income earner than the other, you may want to have the higher income earner delay until age 70. By doing so, if the higher income earner pre-deceases the other spouse, the surviving spouse will move up to the higher benefit level for their remaining lifetime.

4. A spouse can begin taking their own benefit (based on their own record) and then switch to a spousal benefit if it is higher once the higher earning spouse begins taking their benefit. Please note if the lower earning spouse takes their own benefits prior to Full Retirement Age (FRA), then they will have a permanent reduction of their Spousal social security benefits. For example, if Jill begins her own benefits at 62 and waits for Jack to obtain age 66 (his FRA) and plans to switch to the spousal benefit, Jill will receive 50% of Jack's less any discounts for taking her benefit early.

5. If you plan to continue working and earning over the level of the earning test limits, it would likely make sense to delay taking Social Security benefits until you are no longer earning income over the earning test limits or reach FRA, and therefore are no longer subject to an earnings test.

6. Do you need income now and have little other sources to pull from or do you need income and have minimal sources that would keep your income tax at a low level?

The break-even question:

People always want to know how long must you live to get the same amount of benefits if you claim at different ages. If you take benefits at 62 (assuming you are no longer earning other income and it makes financial to do so) or you take benefits at 66 or 70, how long must you live for all the numbers to provide you the same total dollars of benefits. The graph below illustrates the crossover points. They all begin to crossover between the late 70's and early 80's. Keep in mind this is simply the total benefits received, not receiving the amounts and reinvesting the dollars into something earning, "x" percent. This illustration assumes you utilize the dollars and simply want to know when all the dollars received are the same.

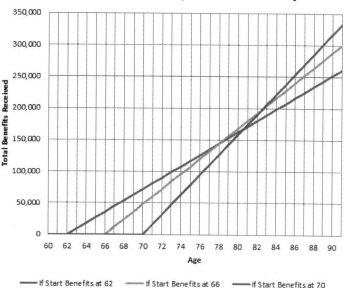

Standard Social Security Breakeven Analysis

---If Start Benefits at 62   ---If Start Benefits at 66   ---If Start Benefits at 70

Two advanced strategies:

I will comment briefly on two advanced planning strategies. These are the File and Suspend strategy and Restricted Application strategy. There are substantial changes that went into effect in 2016 due to the bipartisan budget act of 2015.

The File and Suspend strategy allowed a spousal benefit to be taken on a retiree's benefit record while the retiree's benefit continued to accrue until taken at the maximum level at age 70. This strategy has been eliminated unless it was elected by April 30, 2016.

Restricted application will allow one spouse to take a spousal benefit equal to 50% of the spouse they are claiming on and then be allowed to switch to their own benefit at a time in the future. This strategy can best be illustrated by way of example.

Restricted Application Example:

- Jack is 66 (Born in 1953 or earlier)
- Jill is 66
- Jack PIA is $1,800 and age 70 benefit is $2,400
- Jill PIA is $800, and age 70 benefit is $1,100
- Jack could file and take own benefit and Jill could claim spousal benefit
  o $1,800 to Jack
  o $900 to Jill

- Restricted Application would allow:
  o Jill to file for own benefit of $800/month
  o Jack could file a Restricted Application for 50% of Spouses benefit, $400/month (since Jack didn't file for his own benefit, it will accrue delayed retirement credits)
  o Monthly benefits of $1,200 between 66-70
  o At age 70, Jack will switch to his max benefit of $2,400 per month and Jill will switch to spousal

benefit of Jack which is 50% of PIA or $900
o Monthly benefits of $3,300 from 70 and beyond
o If Jack pre-deceases Jill, she will step up to age 70 benefit for the rest of her life

The Restricted Application strategy is only available to those that are born in 1953 or earlier. The restricted application allows for a retiree to take a restricted application of spousal benefits while allowing their own benefit to continue to increase until you switch to your own benefit.

Social Security Recap:

Social Security is the core of retirement income for many retirees. The key to planning is to understand your personal situation and how the various options relate to your unique situation. Everyone's situation is going to be unique and will require personalized planning to identify the optimal solution.

Required Minimum Distribution (RMD):

The IRS has a way to assist with helping you fill your Income Gap… they require distributions to begin from your tax-deferred retirement accounts by age 70.5. Here are the key things you need to know when it comes to RMD's.

What are they?

RMD's are simply the minimum amount that the IRS requires you to take from your tax-deferred retirement accounts. These would be 401k's, IRA's, 403b's. Basically, any retirement account except a Roth IRA.

When do they begin?

RMD's begin the year that you turn age 70.5. The very first RMD can be delayed up until April 1 of the following year, instead of having to take it out by December 31 of the current year (as all future RMD's will be required in the future).

Here is an example: if your birthday is May 1st, 1946, then you would turn 70.5 in 2016. You can delay your very first RMD until age April 1, 2017. All future RMD's must be taken by December 31. If you delay the first RMD, you will be required to take the first by April 1, 2017, and take the second RMD by December 31.

How is it calculated?

Your RMD is calculated based on the prior year end value of your tax-deferred retirement account and using a factor based on life expectancy that is provided by the IRS[10]. This table is used as long as your spouse is not more than 10 years younger than you. If that is the case, there is a separate table with factors that will be used.

Example of RMD calculation:

Back to our example of turning 70.5 in 2016, if you had an IRA balance of $1,000,000 on 12/31/15, then you would take $1,000,000 and divide that by the first factor which is 27.4. This would provide the RMD amount of $36,496.35 required to be taken out of the account by 12/31/16 (or

[10]https://www.irs.gov/pub/irs-tege/uniform_rmd_wksht.pdf

technically can be delayed until April 1, 2017).

RMD quirks:

There are a few quirky parts to RMD's. Here are a few things to be mindful of regarding RMD's.

- You can take out the total amount of your RMD that would be due across multiple IRA's through one IRA. For example: if you have four IRA's that total $1,000,000, you could take the total RMD required out of one IRA if it meets the total RMD required.
- You cannot aggregate across different types of accounts. For instance, you cannot take the RMD due from IRA's, from a 401k or vice versa.
- You cannot take your spouse's RMD by withdrawing from your accounts.
- The penalty for not taking out your RMD is significant. It is 50% of your RMD level, and you still must take out your RMD!
- Your RMD must come out of your tax-deferred account, but it doesn't require you to spend the money. You can reinvest the funds into other investments.

There are several things to know and understand with RMD's so that you can plan properly and use them advantageously to fill your income gap in retirement.

Getting the next generation to understand the Stretch IRA:

When you pass (perhaps you and your spouse) and your children or someone else inherits your IRA, it is important that they understand their withdrawal options from the IRA.

They typically have three options.

1. Take the amount of the account in full right away.
2. Take the amount of the account in full by the end of five years.
3. Take the Required Minimum Distribution over your life expectancy from the RMD each year.

Option #1 - Take the amount of the account in full right away:

With this option your heirs will receive the account in full right away. They will be responsible for ordinary income taxes owed on the distribution amount. There is no penalty, since these are distributions due to death, but there are normal Federal and state income taxes due.

Option #2 - Take the amount of the account in full by the end of five years:

Similar to option #1, but with the plan to distribute the full amount over five years. Taxes will be owed, no penalty is due, and all funds must be distributed within five years. This will be helpful from an influx of cash stand point, but will take a significant tax hit right away.

Option #3 - Take the Required Minimum Distribution (RMD) over your life expectancy from the RMD each year.

Just as you would take RMD's over your lifetime after age 70.5, the same is true for the beneficiary of an inherited account. They will need to withdraw a small minimal amount out of their IRA each and every year. By doing so they can continue to stretch out the tax and time period in which the tax is owed. The term Stretch IRA is simply a marketing term, but its impact does hold true with limiting the tax liability to a minimum each and every year compared to withdrawing the full amount right away or over a five year period.

Pension options — if you're that lucky:

I'm always a little nervous when I talk about pensions in the Retirement Planning Blueprint® classes. It's not because the material is difficult to know or understand, but simply because pensions are polarizing. If I have a class of twenty households, there is a chance about 25% will have a pension. The other 75% will have to rely solely on Social Security and their own investment success, while the other 25% will be able to rely more on guaranteed income between Social Security and pension income.

If you are one of the few that have pension income options, you will need to make some decisions when it comes to starting your pension. Here are a few of the decisions that most plans will provide when it comes to determining how to take your monthly income:

1. Single Life only
2. 100% Joint Life survivor
3. 75% Joint Life survivor
4. 50% Joint Life survivor

Single Life Only – This option will only provide for a pension payment while the worker that earned the pension is living. As soon as the worker passes away, the pension payments will cease. If you are married, electing this option will often require the spouse to sign off and elect this option with the working spouse.

Joint Life survivor options – These options are all similar, except for the amount that will continue to be paid to the surviving spouse. Most plans will provide multiple remaining payment percentages ranging from 100% to 50%. For example, if the pension payment is $1,000 and there is a 100% Joint Life payout then the remaining payment will continue at $1,000. At a 75% survivor payment, it would be reduced to $750, and at 50% it would be $500. What will usually occur, is that a higher monthly payment is paid while the working spouse is still alive if a lower joint life payment is elected, and less of a monthly payment is paid if the higher monthly remaining payment is elected.

Thoughts on Cash Balance Plans:

Cash Balance plans are a hybrid between an account that has a lump sum value and a monthly payment option. These accounts typically have a crediting formula based on annual interest credits, regardless of market performance, and additional credits may be made based on age and years of service. These have largely replaced the traditional pension plans.

When you leave an employer, you have a few options (sometimes pending age requirements) of what to do with your cash balance plans:

1. Take it in a lump sum
2. Roll it over to an IRA
3. Leave it where it's at for now

4. Take a monthly payout

Each of these options are helpful for each unique situation and here are some big picture thoughts on these options:

Take it in a lump sum:

Taking the lump sum will create ordinary income tax owed on any part that is distributed outright to you. This is likely the least favorable option, unless you are really strapped for cash.

Roll it over to an IRA:

You can transfer the lump sum balance to an IRA without tax or penalty. This may be a preferred option if you want to try to out earn the amount of interest credited on an annual basis. This will require a level of risk to achieve that your current plan does not require, but if you have a long-term time horizon it could make sense.

Leave it where it's at for now:

Leaving the plan in place may be an option. You will need to spend time evaluating the guaranteed interest credits and compare that to your overall investment mix and appetite for risk to try and outpace those levels.

Take a monthly payout:

If you have reached any age requirements that the plan contains, you may be able to take a monthly income payout. These options are typically similar to the pension payout options we addressed earlier. Any dollars paid will create ordinary income tax on your tax return each year. To identify whether it seems better to take the income payouts or invest the funds in an IRA for longer term growth, you will need to understand the payment amounts in relation to the lump sum balance. You should understand the risk required to reach certain investment goals to achieve higher returns than would be comparative to the payout levels of the monthly income options. If the monthly payments are significantly higher than what a reasonable investment return could provide (and you don't need the liquidity), then it may make sense to take the monthly payments. If the monthly payments are lower than what a reasonable conservative return would provide, then you may want to take a lump sum, invest the proceeds and take your own distributions from the portfolio.

4

THE RETIREMENT INVESTMENT PLAN

Are you planning for your investments in light of retirement?

In 1953, Sir Edmund Hillary was the first to successfully go up to the top of Mt. Everest and make it back down. It's interesting to phrase his success in that manner, because he is the first that is known to have made it up and back down successfully. Every year there are hundreds who successfully scale Mt. Everest, yet there are 15-20 who die on Everest every year. Very few die on the way up the Mountain, in fact only about 15% die on the way up, but 85% die on the way down.

The story of Everest and the perils that can come more often from the way down than the way up is parallel to entering retirement for an investor. For so many years, future retirees have simply saved money over a long period of time. When you are saving in your 30's and 40's or even early 50's, you can simply do most anything with your investments, and as long as it is in the markets and you do not take it out, you will have more later than you started with. Living through ups and downs in the markets is fairly easy to do, because time continues to be on your side.

Accumulation vs. Decumulation:

The significant difference between saving and investing in your 30's, 40's and 50's compared to your retirement years, is that during your working and earning years, you are constantly accumulating into the portfolio. This changes completely when you reach retirement and begin withdrawing from the portfolio. No longer can you save in peace knowing that time is on your side. As we've seen the retirement period for many may encompass 30+ years, so there is a lot of time to make sure your money lasts, but the way in which you invest your money is much different as you enter the decumulation years of your portfolio.

In my retirement classes I tell the story of three friends, that were all the same age, started with the same amount of money invested and earned the same average return over their working years. At the end of 25 working years, even though they all had different investment returns in different years (two of the three have the same returns, but just in different years), the returns all averaged out to the same 7% return, and they all ended up with the same amount of money at the end of 25 years at their retirement party when they were 65 years old.

Now, they enter their retirement and decumulation years of the portfolio. Like before, they all have the same average returns and two of the three have the exact same returns (just in different years). Their hope is to fund retirement until at least age 90. Over the next 25 years, two have a high amount remaining at the end of the 25-year period (one actually has over twice as much as the other), while one has zero investable assets remaining by age 88[11].

What is the difference between the three you wonder? It is simply the investment returns that they experienced during their first few years of retirement as they began withdrawing from their portfolio.

This is what many Financial Planners refer to as sequence of returns risk. This is the risk of receiving lower or negative returns early in a period when withdrawals are made from an individual's investments[12].

We will spend time later in this section addressing how to mitigate this sequence of returns risk. The key is to have a plan in place that meets your needs from the portfolio to meet your income gap, while lowering the sequence of returns risk as a new retiree.

One key to successful investing as a retiree:

As I've worked with hundreds of retirees over the past decade, having lived through the Great Recession of 2008, I've learned there is one key to a retiree having peace with their investment strategy. That key is to not lose a lot of money!

---

[11]https://www.blackrock.com/pt/literature/investor-education/sequence-of-returns-one-pager-va-us.pd
[12]http://www.investopedia.com/terms/s/sequence-risk.asp

This becomes a lot more relevant if we look at the cruel math of investment losses. To illustrate this, let's look at some potential losses for an investment portfolio.

An all stock portfolio in their worst year would have been down over 40%[13].

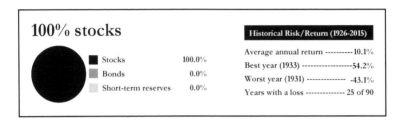

Even a balanced portfolio of 60% stocks and 40% bonds would have been down over 25% in their worst year.

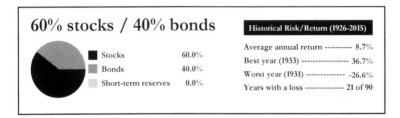

A very conservative portfolio of 30% stocks and 70% bonds would have been down nearly 15% in their worst year.

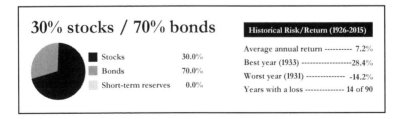

[13]https://personal.vanguard.com/us/insights/saving-investing/model-portfolio-allocations (see website for specific stock and bond allocations)

If you lost 40% on paper in stocks, then the big question becomes how much you need to make back to get to breakeven. Well, the answer can be enlightening, but also concerning. A 40% loss would require a 66.7% positive return just to breakeven[14].

A 25% loss would require a gain of 33.3% to breakeven, and a loss of 15% would require a gain of almost 18% to breakeven. As you can see, when it comes to losing a high percentage of your investments, it requires a lot of positive performance to get back to where you started.

As we go down the path of establishing a proper investment plan for your retirement years, I must state something very important when it comes to establishing an investment strategy. There simply is no silver bullet! There are many opinions and options on how to do this most effectively. I will lay out a few strategies that you can consider learning more about to see which best fits your personal situation.

Keys to investing:
* Know your tools
* Understand techniques
* Devise a strategy
* Stick to your strategy

Know your tools:

When I teach the Retirement Planning Blueprint® at local Colleges, I have a wide array of people with various investment backgrounds in class. To ensure everyone is on

14http://shurwest.com/wp-content/uploads/2013/08/The-Math-of-Gains-Losses.pdf

the same page, I will begin with a very high level overview of the tools available to invest and use as a part of your investment strategy.

The key to building an effective investment strategy is to understand what you own and what your options are. For most everyone the common tools will be:

- Bonds
- Stocks
- Mutual Funds
- Exchange Traded Funds (ETFs)
- Annuities

We will go into depth on each of these tools:

Bonds:

Bonds are an IOU that you have been given from someone that you loaned money to. You can buy a bond of a Corporation (think Apple, Microsoft, any other large corporation), a Government (think the US Government, Germany, any other Country), or a local municipality (think your State or local City).

When you give this Corporation, Government, or Municipality money, you are a lender to them. They are providing you with a stated level of return over a defined period of time.

With bonds there are a few key things to understand when it comes to increasing the return of bonds. Bonds at their core are meant to provide the stated level of return over a defined time period. There can be appreciation or depreciation on the bonds, dependent on the interest rate environment in which they were purchased in and the current interest rate environment. This is commonly referred to as the inverse relationship of interest rates and bond prices.

If interest rates rise:

Yields Rise

Prices Fall

If interest rates fall:

Prices Rise

Yields Fall

For example: if you purchased a 10 year Government bond at the beginning of the year that is scheduled to pay you 2% over the next 10 years and a year later new 10 year Government bonds are only paying 1.5% then the bond you bought that is paying 2% is a much better bond to own, and therefore, would likely have appreciated in price. The opposite is also true that if you purchased a bond and now new bonds are paying higher rates, there is a good chance that your bond on paper is now worth less.

The defined return and timeframe presents an interesting situation for bond investors. Ultimately, if you own an actual bond from an issuer, then you can always hold that bond until it has fully matured, and then you will receive the principal that you initially placed into the bond back at the end of the term. This is a little advanced and different from how most people own bonds today, which is in mutual funds or exchange traded funds, in which you have virtually no control of bonds being bought or sold before maturity.

To increase the return or the yield on bonds there are really two ways to accomplish this and both carry higher levels of risk. The first option is to increase the term or duration before the bond is set to mature, and the second is to buy bonds with lower credit quality.

You can purchase bonds that mature in a year all the way out to thirty years (or potentially longer). The longer you allow the borrower to use your funds, the more it will cost them in the way of interest back to you. The risk you carry is whether or not the lender will still be around in 30 years or whatever term you invest in.

The second way to enhance returns in bonds is to purchase lower quality bonds. Every issuer is rated by outside agencies and are given a grade of their credit worthiness. This can be as high as AAA and as low as CCC. The lower you go, the higher interest you would receive. The risk for the lender (you) is the fact that the lower credit rating the closer the company may be to default. If the company defaults, it is likely you will receive nothing back for what you initially put into the investment.

A final risk for owning longer term bonds is the inflation risk associated with locking in low interest rates. If you own bonds that have a long time before they mature and inflation picks up, unless you want to take a loss, you may need to continue holding onto bonds that are not paying a rate that keeps up with current inflation levels.

With bond investing, the key risks, as we've discussed are the interest rate risk, business risk, and inflation risk. These are the risks of owning bonds. There are certainly benefits as well.

For a retiree a bond can provide a specific level of return. This can provide predictable cash flow and income for the retiree. If the retiree owns US Government bonds or Investment Grade Corporate Bonds, they can have a fairly high degree of certainty that the bond will continue to pay the stated rate of return until maturity. US Government bonds have no default risk and Investment Grade Corporate Bonds carry very little default risk.

Even though bonds can have volatility with appreciation and deprecation, they tend to perform well during stock market declines. This is why conservative portfolios own more bonds than more aggressive portfolios.

Stocks:

The next most common tool in the investment tool box is stocks. Unlike bonds where you are a lender receiving a stated rate of return, by investing in the stock of a company you are an owner in the company. By becoming an owner in a company, you are hopeful for the company to perform well and provide you with appreciation by way of the stock price going up over time. You may also receive cash from the company in the form of dividends.

There are various kinds of stocks of companies to invest into: you can invest in large company stocks (such as Fortune 500 companies), smaller companies, International companies, and Emerging Markets (smaller country companies).

The risk of investing in a company is the chance that the company ceases to exist at some point. While fairly uncommon for large companies, it can certainly happen. This is the key reason it is prudent to invest in more than one company, or even a dozen companies. Spreading out the risk among many companies will lower the risk that all of your dollars in one company would be lost if that one company went bankrupt. This is referred to as diversification, and we will discuss this technique as we look at mutual funds and exchange traded funds as investment tools.

How to own stocks and bonds:

The most common form of owning stocks and bonds is through Mutual Funds and Exchange Traded Funds. They are very common with just a few differences. Let's look at Mutual Funds first.

Mutual Funds:

A mutual fund is a basket of stocks or bonds (sometimes both) that are managed by way of a common strategy. For instance, you can own a large cap stock fund that will own all large cap stocks. By owning that one fund, you may now own 100, 500, 1000, or even 5000 companies. You can buy a mutual fund that has holdings in large companies, small, international, or any combination. It could own stocks, bonds, or both. Mutual funds provide diversification and some can have active management or passive management. Active management funds have underlying fund managers that are attempting to buy and sell stocks or bonds at opportune times to enhance performance while passive managers are attempting to replicate the index or benchmark that the fund is trying to match.

Mutual funds are simple to own: you can purchase through your retirement plans, in an IRA, or after-tax investment account at a brokerage company. Mutual funds are only bought and sold at the end of business each day at 4pm. They do not have an intraday value. The price is set at the end of each day.

Exchange Traded Funds (ETF's):

ETF's carry many of the same characteristics that Mutual Funds carry, with one significant difference, which is that they can trade intraday. You can buy an ETF at 9:30am at the market open and sell it at 9:31am after owning for a minute. With a mutual fund, the fund could not be sold until 4:00pm market close.

ETF's are created to adhere to a certain investment strategy, again large stocks, small stocks, International companies, etc. One other difference with ETF's is that they are easier to create, so there are more available that may have a more exotic type strategy. For instance, it may be difficult to find a Mutual Fund with exposure to North African Gold Miners, while an ETF may be available with that strategy in place.

Owning stocks and bonds outside of funds:

Stocks and bonds can always be owned individually and not inside the shell of mutual funds or ETF's. The benefits of doing so is that you will forgo the underlying expense ratios of the funds (these are the expenses that you pay to the fund manager for ongoing management).

The issue with purchasing stocks and bonds outside of funds is that unless you have enough investment dollars to put into enough stocks and bonds, you may not have a strong level of diversification in place. If you have enough capital to put towards enough individual stocks and bonds, owning investments this way could make sense.

Annuities:

Annuities can be a four-letter word to some, and the greatest investment option ever created for others. The interesting part is that an annuity is actually an insurance product sold by insurance companies and not technically investment products (well all except the variable annuity, which is an investment in an insurance wrapper).

Annuities come in many different shapes and sizes, I will give an annuity 101 here.

Main annuity types:

There are four main annuity types:
- Income Annuity
- Fixed Annuity
- Fixed Index Annuity
- Variable Annuity

Income Annuity:

The income annuity is a fairly simple product. It is designed to provide income at some point. The income annuity can provide income right away, which is known as the immediate income annuity, or it can be set up to provide income at a future defined date, which is known as the deferred income annuity.

The income annuity is simply exchanging a lump sum amount of money for a contractual agreement with an insurance company for a defined amount of income for a defined period of time.

For example, an immediate annuity purchased by a 65 year old male with a joint life payout (which covers the spouse as well) could be set up so that income is paid for the life of the husband and wife. No matter what, they will receive a specific dollar amount for the rest of their lives. If they hand over $100,000 they may receive $5,000 per year for the rest of their joint lives.

These types of products can be structured in many different ways. If more income is desired, then you could decide to only have a percentage paid out to the surviving spouse (such as 50% or 75%). You could put into place a defined time period, such as 10 years, but if both spouses pass away, then the heirs receive nothing afterwards. Likewise, if you desire to have increasing income to keep up with inflation, you can take a lower initial payout in exchange for Cost of Living Adjustments. If you want to place a death benefit on the annuity if both spouses pass away and there is concern that the funds that haven't been used will not pass to the heirs, then a death benefit will take away this concern. There are many things that can be added or taken off these types of annuities to align it with your wishes, but certainly understand the more bells and whistles and options added will lower the monthly payouts.

Fixed Annuity:

A fixed annuity is a very simply product. It works very similarly to a CD or a bond. The annuity has a defined time period with a defined level of interest paid to the purchaser. For example, if you purchased a 5 year Fixed Annuity that is paying 2%, you would receive 2% each year for 5 years and the initial amount you put into the annuity at the end of the 5 year period.

These types of annuities mimic bonds or CD's in that the longer the term period the better payout. As well, the lower rated insurance companies may provide higher paying fixed annuities than the higher rated insurance companies.

Fixed Index Annuity (FIA):

The FIA is a little newer to the market with a history only dating back to the mid 1990's. These were developed to compete with CD rates and potentially short-term bond rates. Their intention and invention were not created to compete with the returns of stocks. They have a number of interesting characteristics that much be understood before placing dollars into these contracts. Here are some of them:

FIA – the basics:

The FIA at its core is a Fixed Annuity option which simply means it comes with a Principal Guarantee. This is very appealing to many conservative retirees. The index part is where it can become a little confusing and is different from other annuity options. The index part means that the dollars invested in these annuities can be allocated to various indexes, that if they go up, you may participate in some or all of the gains, sometimes only up to a capped level.

Here is an example: If an FIA has an indexed strategy that is tied to the S&P 500, it may state that you receive whatever the price increase is in the S&P 500 index up to 3%. Over the next year, if the S&P 500 goes up 10%, you will receive 3%. However, if the S&P 500 goes down by 20%, you will not lose a penny. You can have limited gains, but experience no downside risk. This is appealing to some conservative investors, but it is important again to state the returns for these sort of options will compete with CD's and short-term bonds, but shouldn't be seen as a replacement for stock market returns. This is simply an example of how a Fixed Index Annuity would be constructed, there are some that may have uncapped strategies that give the potential for an account owner to earn higher levels of return.

FIA – advanced:

FIA's also have appeal in that the positive returns that are created at the end of each 12 month period, are locked into place in the value of the account. For example, if you earned 4% on your $100,000 and that equates to $4,000, which now brings your total amount to $104,000, your balance will never go below $104,000 (as long as you have no withdrawals and rider expenses).

FIA's can also have lifetime withdrawal benefits (sometimes for a fee or built into the product). These types of benefits allow for the FIA to grow a hypothetical bucket (often referred to as the income bucket) that can be used to withdrawal income off of in retirement…similar to an immediate or deferred income annuity.

FIA – cons to know:

In general, the biggest con about owning an FIA is that it is likely to have a surrender period, typically of around 10 years. This means if you place money into an FIA and need all the money back out one year from now, you may be accessed a penalty for taking it all out before the end of the surrender period. Most contracts allow a 10% annual withdrawal of what was initially put into the account, without penalty. It is important to not put all of your investment capital into something such as this, due to this lack of liquidity.

Any time we are talking about investing it is important to understand the fees. Most FIA's have the fees built into the return expectations of the FIA. For instance, the fee is already accounted for in the performance range that is likely for an FIA; there are not fees that will detract from the account performance. Some will sell these sorts of products and entertain the idea that there are no fees. That is simply unfair to state; everything will always have some sort of fee. There isn't a fee that will detract from the account balance, but there is a fee that will limit the upside performance of your account.

These products can make sense for someone looking for a principal guaranteed option that may provide higher returns than CD's, short-term bonds, and cash.

Variable Annuities:

Variable annuities are a complex insurance product as they are a hybrid insurance and investment product. You obtain these from insurance companies, but you invest in underlying investment options like stock and bond mutual funds. Variable annuities can provide some of the lifetime income benefits like FIA's. There are no guarantees, so if you have a bad year with your investment options, you may lose money.

As well, fees are taken away from the performance of the annuity. The variable annuity may make sense for someone that is looking for lifetime income benefits and is okay with potential loss of principal.

Four Outcomes:

Now that we've completed are review of the tools available to place our hard-earned money into as a place to try and earn a return, let's now place them into Four unique categories that I call the Four Outcomes. Below is a chart that I provide in the Retirement Planning Blueprint® class to illustrate these Four Outcomes.

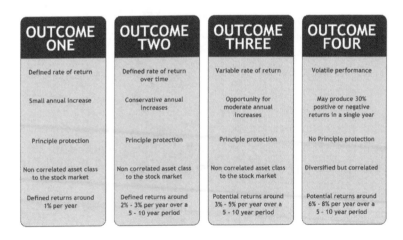

OUTCOME ONE	OUTCOME TWO	OUTCOME THREE	OUTCOME FOUR
Defined rate of return	Defined rate of return over time	Variable rate of return	Volatile performance
Small annual increase	Conservative annual increases	Opportunity for moderate annual increases	May produce 30% positive or negative returns in a single year
Principle protection	Principle protection	Principle protection	No Principle protection
Non correlated asset class to the stock market	Non correlated asset class to the stock market	Non correlated asset class to the stock market	Diversified but correlated
Defined returns around 1% per year	Defined returns around 2% - 3% per year over a 5 - 10 year period	Potential returns around 3% - 5% per year over a 5 - 10 year period	Potential returns around 6% - 8% per year over a 5 - 10 year period

What goes where?

Outcome One consists of Principal protection items that have 100% liquidity, these would include:
- Bank Accounts
- Short-Term CD's that allow for withdrawals

Outcome Two consists of Principal protection options that have longer maturities than Outcome One items. If held to maturity (and no defaults) Outcome Two will provide a specific stated level of return. These items should produce a higher rate of return than Outcome One. These would include:
- Mid-Term CD's
- Long-Term CD's
- Fixed Annuities
- Individual Bonds

Outcome Three consists of Principal protection options that do not provide specific levels of return, but do provide the potential for better levels of return than Outcomes One or Two. They likely have terms of 5-10 years (potentially longer). These will provide principal guarantee with the opportunity for conservative increases over time. The cons are that access to capital (ie. Liquidity) is likely limited during the initial term period for these types of options. These would include:
- Market Linked CD's
- Fixed Index Annuities
- Structured Notes (to an extent, understand if principal losses can occur)

Outcome Four provides no principle protection. This category over time should (typically) produce the highest levels of returns. Risk is the significant difference between this category and other categories. Anything in this Outcome could lose a portion of principal over the short-term, mid-term or long-term. This category would include the following:

- Stocks
- Bond Funds
- Mutual Funds
- Exchange Traded Funds
- Asset Allocation Funds
- Target Date Funds

By better understanding your tools and the potential outcomes of the tools, you should be able to create an investment plan that better aligns with your goals, objective and risk tolerance.

Techniques:

Now that we are aware of the tools available for your investment dollars, the next step is to understand the various techniques available to prudently invest.

Here are some of the ones that we will discuss in detail:

- The principal of diversification
- Understand the relationship between risk and return
- Understanding that time matters

The principal of diversification:

We have all heard the quote to not put all your eggs in one basket. This is a prudent tenant of investing. Diversification provides protection against the concentrated and magnified risk of having everything you own invested in one, two, or a few companies. This is also true even for investing in bonds outside of Government bonds, as any corporation is subject to potential default at some point in the history of their company.

Diversification is not without risk. If you own a large cap mutual fund with 500 stocks inside of it and 450 of them are down for the year (think 2008), then you will still have a fund that loses money for the year. However, it will protect you from owning one stock and having to endure a potential complete loss. Diversification can be accomplished through owning mutual funds, exchange traded funds, or buying enough individual stocks and bonds to create a diversified portfolio.

Diversification also allows you to take advantage of various asset classes and to not have only one that performs well (or bad). For instance, some years US large stocks will outperform Emerging Markets, while other years, US small stocks will be the best performing asset class. Diversifying across all asset classes will provide the benefit of taking part in some of the upside of all the asset classes. To illustrate the benefits of diversification, here is a chart that shows how no one asset class outperforms every single year. This is called a Callan[15] chart and outlines the best to worst performing asset class for each year.

The Callan Periodic Table of Investment Returns

Annual Returns for Key Indices Ranked in Order of Performance (1996–2015)

1996	1997	1998	1999	2000	2001	2002	2003	2004	2005	2006	2007	2008	2009	2010	2011	2012	2013	2014	2015

---

[15]https://www.callan.com/research/periodic/

Risk & Return are related:

As we've reviewed, historically, stocks are riskier than bonds and conversely bonds are safer than stocks. Intuitively, we can understand that risk and return are intricately related. The more risk you are willing to take, the greater potential return your portfolio may be able to achieve. Likewise, the less risk you are willing to take, the lower potential return you are likely to achieve. There are certainly anomalies where a historically low risk portfolio will outperform a high-risk portfolio on a short-term snapshot, but historically over long periods of time, these rules of risk and return will hold true. To illustrate this tenant, here is some information from Vanguard[16] that shows the wide disparity over a one year basis for a 100% stock and 0% bond portfolio down to a 0% stock and 100% bond portfolio.

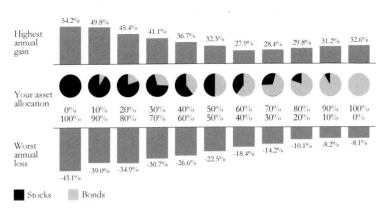

Source: Vanguard. Best and worst calendar year returns from 1926 through 2014. Stocks are represented by the Standard & Poor's 90 Index from 1926 to March 3, 1957; the S&P 500 Index from March 4, 1957, through 1974; the Wilshire 5000 Index from 1975 through April 22, 2005; the MSCI US Broad Market Index from April 23, 2005, to June 2, 2013; and the CRSP US Total Market Index thereafter. Bonds are represented by the S&P High Grade Corporate Index from 1926 to 1968; the Citigroup High Grade Index from 1969 to 1972; the Barclays U.S. Long Credit AA Index from 1973 to 1975; the Barclays U.S. Aggregate Bond Index from 1976 to 2009; and the Spliced Barclays U.S. Aggregate Float Adjusted Index thereafter.

---

[16]https://investor.vanguard.com/investing/how-to-invest/investment-risk

As you can see, the worst and best one years for a 100% stock and 0% bonds down to a 0% bonds and 100% stock can vary dramatically. Remembering back to the beginning of this chapter and the cruel math of investment losses, you can understand the impact of being invested 100% in stock can cause a new retiree if they were to experience one of the extreme loss years on the front end of retirement.

Time matters:

Taking the long view is always important when investing. Looking over a long period of time we can begin to see how different allocations between stocks and bonds perform While there can be extreme ups and downs over any one year period, over the long-term, portfolios holding more stock tend to average better returns than portfolios with less stock. Conversely, for a conservative investor, the risk of loss is much lower with less stock while the long-term return expectation over time is lower as well.

Here is a graphic from Vanguard[17] that illustrates how time matters to receive average investment returns over time.

The mixture of assets defines the spectrum of returns:
Best, worst and average returns for various stock/bond allocations, 1926–2013

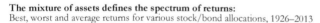

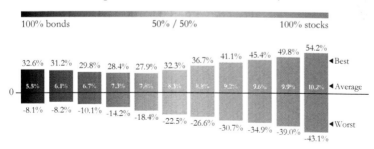

Note: Stocks are represented by the Standard & Poor's 90 Index from 1926 to March 3, 1957; the S&P 500 Index from March 4, 1957, through 1974; the Wilshire 5000 Index from 1975 through April 22, 2005; and the MSCI US Broad Market Index thereafter. Bonds are represented by the S&P High Grade Corporate Index from 1926 to 1968; the Citigroup High Grade Index from 1969 to 1972; the Barclays U.S. Long Credit AA Index from 1973 to 1975; and the Barclays U.S. Aggregate Bond Index thereafter. Data are through December 31, 2013. Source: Vanguard.

---

[17] https://personal.vanguard.com/us/insights/investingtruths/investing-truth-about-risk

As you can see, there is a wide disparity across the spectrum with investment returns of stocks and bonds and balanced portfolios in between. The key to holding any investment is to ensure time remains on your side to ensure that you will be able to live through the extremes without doing anything that could harm your investment performance.

In this next section, we will work through a few strategies that will allow you to have time on your side no matter your age.

How much in stocks and bonds?

Now we must determine how to allocate between stocks and bonds or said another way, determine how much risk to take in our portfolios, and how to allocate across stocks, bonds or annuities.

Here are a few ways to identify at a very high level how much to hold in stocks and how much in bonds:
- Emotional
  o Risk Tolerance
  o Understand max loss that you can accept
- Financial Planning
  o Understand the return level that is needed to make your long-term retirement plan work
  o Understand your Time horizon and cash flow needs from the portfolio
- Rules of thumb
  o Review Rule of 100
  o Target Date Retirement Funds

To break these down deeper, here are the details:

Emotional:

There is always an inherent emotional part to investing. Your portfolio value will go up and it will go down. Even in holding a conservative portfolio with more bonds than stocks, there is a chance you will experience a double digit negative year. This can take its toll on an investor, especially an investor that has recently retired. To help identify how much to hold in stocks and how much to hold in bonds a Risk Tolerance Questionnaire can be helpful. There are many different ones out there, and they should all help get you to the same place, which is to be made aware of where it seems your max pain point in terms of investment loss would take place. For some, this may be a negative return of 10%, others maybe it is 25%. This is certainly only a starting point, but if you do nothing else, it would be helpful to ensure you do not have an excessive level of risk in your portfolio.

One item to note as we talk about negatives and worst years in history for an investment mix, one thing to keep in mind is that if you can hold on and not make a decision to sell out of investments at a loss, then historically you should be able to rebound back to where you started within a few years[18].

Guides:

A couple guides, if you do nothing else, is to look at the rule of 100 and Target Date Retirement funds. The rule of 100 has been around as a rule of thumb for a long time. What it states is that the amount you have in stocks should not

---

[18]https://blog.wealthfront.com/no-need-to-fear-market-corrections/

be more than 100 minus your age. If you are 60 years old, then you shouldn't have more than 40% (100 minus 60) in stocks. If you are a 40-year-old investor, then you would have no more than 60% in stocks. This guide can be helpful in preventing too much stock risk in a portfolio for a retiree. It has received mixed review in the current investment atmosphere as the interest received on higher quality bonds are so low.

Today, some would argue to use the rule of 110 or even 120. Whereas a 60-year-old with the rule of 110 would have 50% in stocks and (110 minus 60) and 60% with the rule of 120. Either way, the rule of thumb is helpful to ensure not too much is being held in stocks which can have a materially negative impact for new retirees.

A second rule of thumb that will serve as a guide to making the decision around stocks and bonds is to review the allocations of Target Date Retirement funds. If you are 60 today and planning to retire at 65, you could look at a 2020 Target Date Retirement fund and see what the allocation between stocks and bonds would be. For instance, reviewing the Vanguard 2020 Target Date Retirement Fund[19] currently

holds 57% in stocks and 43% in bonds. For a 60 year old, this would be in between the rule of 110 and 120.

These are certainly only guides, but can be helpful to ensure an exorbitant amount of risk is not being taken on by a retiree. Let's now examine a deeper way to set up your stock and bond mix.

---

[19]https://personal.vanguard.com/us/funds/snapshot?FundId=0682&FundIntExt=INT#tab=2

Financial Planning:

The Financial Planning approach requires identifying the actual cash flow needs you will have from your portfolio and building a strategy within your investment portfolio to meet those requirements. This will require spending time to identify your income gap we discussed in chapter one.

To identify your income gap, we will first calculate your total guaranteed income sources in retirement. For most this would be Social Security benefits for the retiree and Social Security benefits for the second retiree, or 50% of the retirees benefits as the spousal benefit. Some others may have a pension from a previous corporate career or from being a Government employee. After identifying the guaranteed income sources, you will need to take time to assess what your expenses are likely to be in retirement. Add a buffer to this figure and then figure out what your income gap is estimated to be. An example would look something like this:

Retiree Social Security benefit of $2,500 per month, Spousal benefit at $1,250 per month. No pensions to include. Expenses are estimated to be $5,000 per month with a 10% buffer would bring that up to right at $5,500 per month.

The income gap is therefore estimated to be $1,750 per month or $21,000 per year. This figure helps us understand a few things. It helps us understand what you may need on an annual basis from the portfolio and from there we can extrapolate out how to keep time on your side by ensuring a portion remains in bonds to meet the income needs from the portfolio. To be conservative, you may want to place at least 10 years of expected withdrawals into your bond bucket so that the next 10 years of withdrawals are not in stocks, which can have wide swings (good and bad). In this case, if you needed $21,000 per year from the portfolio, then you may want to place $210,000 into the bond bucket. The remaining amount can be invested in stocks for longer term return and to replenish your bond bucket after you take withdrawals from that bucket.

A second component of using Financial Planning to determine your stock and bond allocation is to identify what level of return is needed to fund your long-term retirement plan. This will help you not over allocate to stocks in hopes of higher investment returns if it is not needed to fund your retirement. If a higher level of investment return is needed to fund your retirement, you may want to reevaluate retiring too early if an unrealistic level of investment return is needed, that could require too much risk to be taken to meet the potential investment returns.

Putting it all together:

The big question now becomes how to take everything we've discussed and effectively build an investment strategy that will meet your income gap.

There are number of ways to put this together in a clear, cohesive strategy, and there are a number of opinions on how to do it as well. Here are three strategies to build a strategy for your portfolio.

1. The Total Return Approach
2. The Defined Portfolio Approach
3. The Defined Income Approach

The Total Return Approach:

Let's begin with what I will call the Total Return Approach. The total return approach is the default strategy for most people. This strategy is built by investing in stocks and bonds and holding for the long-term. Your goal is to be a patient investor, diversify your portfolio and believe in historical rates of returns to meet your long-term goals. Your portfolio is seen as one bucket of money and is broken up with a percentage of stocks and bonds. To create your allocation, you can simply use a risk tolerance questionnaire and hold the recommended amount of stocks and bonds.

The pro's:

The total return approach may get you to where you want to go as long as you can stomach market ups and downs and are a patient investor. It is a simple approach and doesn't require a lot of planning outside of understanding your risk tolerance. If you want simplicity, this may be the way to go.

The con's:

The con's to using a total return approach are a couple. First, you will need to have stamina during the ups and downs of the markets. Since your portfolio is simply seen as one bucket of money split between stocks and bonds, you know with certainty that you will see a lot of volatility with this investment mix without a clear strategy to meet your long-term income needs. A second issue is that the allocation you build the day you retire based on your risk tolerance, is not likely the risk tolerance that you will have in two years, and certainly not in ten years. This could be troublesome with potentially more risk than you are comfortable with if you do not reallocate over time.

Defined Portfolio Approach:

The defined portfolio approach uses Financial Planning and your income gap to establish your stock to bond mix. Back to our example earlier in this chapter, if you needed $21,000 from your portfolio, you would place 10 years of cash flow needs from the portfolio into bonds. The bond amount would be $210,000, and the remaining amount could go into stocks. The stock bucket will be much more volatile than the bond bucket, but having 10 years of expected withdrawals in bonds will likely provide much more peace of mind during volatile investment times. On an annual basis the number of withdrawal years that you have in bonds will decrease. On an annual basis, if stocks have been up, you can sell stocks and replenish your bonds back out to a 10 year period of expected withdrawals. If stocks are going through a down cycle, you can continue to use the bonds and wait for stocks to improve before selling and replenishing back out to the 10 year period.

The pro's:

The defined portfolio approach can be effective in creating a strategy that is set to meet defined income needs. This may allow an investor to better weather the ups and downs of market volatility because you know that 10 years of withdrawals are set aside in bonds which historically are less risky than stocks. During volatile stock periods, an investor will likely find it easier to continue withdrawing funds from their investment accounts to meet income needs, whereas it may be difficult to have confidence of pulling funds from their accounts if they are invested in only one bucket without a clear income strategy, as is the case with the total return approach.

The con's:

The major con of the defined portfolio approach is that it does require more work to set up, monitor, and maintain. It will require you to identify what your income needs are from your portfolio and positioning assets accordingly. As time goes on, you will replenish your bond bucket back out to ten years of income needs. By using ten years in the bond bucket, you should be able to weather most market volatility periods. You would sell stocks when they are higher to replenish your bond bucket back out to ten years.

Defined Portfolio Advanced:

One advanced method of the defined portfolio approach is to utilize individual bonds vs. bond funds. Let me explain the difference.

With a bond mutual fund, you are investing into a fund with many other investors, hundreds or thousands of bonds that have various maturities and a mutual fund manager that manages the fund to adhere to a certain investment strategy. This isn't a bad way to invest in bonds, especially if you are in the accumulation phase, but there may be (in my opinion) a slightly better option to meet ongoing income needs for a retiree.

By using individual bonds, (I tend to recommend Government or Government Agency bonds to prevent default risk), you can stagger or ladder maturities of the bonds to meet ongoing cash flow needs. You could set up a similar 10 year amount of cash flow needs from the portfolio in bonds, but in this case you would put the annual cash flow amount needed (i.e., $21,000 in this example) into bonds that would mature each year and meet these needs.

The benefit of building this strategy with individual bonds is that you remove the unknown factors and risk of owning bond mutual funds. As we've reviewed, some bond mutual funds may create losses if companies go bankrupt or if interest rates move up or down, it can have an effect on the funds performance. By using individual Government bonds, you can know specifically what you will receive in interest off the bonds and what the principal amounts will be at the bonds maturities. This can allow you to plan in a more specific manner and build the proper portfolio to meet income needs.

Defined Income Approach:

The defined income approach utilizes an annuity to meet the income gap. Instead of using stocks and bonds and holding a certain amount of each to pull earnings off of to meet your income gap, you can simply purchase an annuity to provide a specific amount of income. This can be set up to buy income immediately or to set up for an income amount at a later time.

For example, using the same income gap example, if you need $1,750 per month, you could look to an insurance company to provide you with an annuity benefit that will meet your income needs. You are replacing a lump sum amount for the income amount that it would provide. This is a good option if you prefer to know that all of your income needs are taken care of and your expected expenses are covered. You can use remaining funds to meet any unexpected or needs beyond your expected expenses.

Pro's:

The pros are that you are able to know your income needs are on an ongoing basis. Your paycheck from the insurance is a contractual guarantee and will continue. This will likely make it easier to maintain your asset allocation and not make unnecessary and harmful investment decisions during volatile market periods.

Cons:

The cons are that you are replacing dollars for income and will lose liquidity for this exchange. You need to ensure you have other funds outside of these to meet any unexpected needs. To exchange a lump sum for income it will require the use of an annuity. As well, to keep up with inflation you will likely have to put more into the annuity. Remember, as we reviewed earlier in this chapter the more bells and whistles you put within the annuity, the less monthly income you will receive.

Recap of Investment Planning:

While there are many opinions and options to build an effective investment plan to meet your income gap, it is important to remember the key is to create a plan that you will be able to stick with in good market environments and challenging markets. You need to understand your risk tolerance, income needs, diversify prudently, keep time on your side, and effectively minimize sequence of returns risk.

5

"You have WHICH healthcare plan?!"

Are you planning for the unexpected with medical and long-term care needs?

For many retirees, their greatest fear in retirement is a severe (and expensive) health care or long-term health care need.

In this section, we will spend time addressing how to mitigate some of these risks and concerns. First, we will start with Medicare for retirees, then address long-term care planning, and lastly spend some time on life insurance.

Medicare:

Medicare came into existence in 1965 to help retirees live into old age with medical insurance. Today, Medicare covers more than 55 million people[20]. Every day, 10,000 people become eligible for Medicare[21]. Medicare has become a staple for most retirees to help plan for their healthcare needs in retirement. The dates, rules and key parts of Medicare can seem complex, so we will begin with the basics.

Medicare basics:

The age to begin Medicare benefits is age 65 for most folks. If you are on Social Security disability, then you will become eligible for Social Security benefits after being on Social Security disability for at least two years.

The eligibility window for your initial sign up for Medicare is three months prior to turning age 65 and three months after turning age 65. During this time, you can sign up for Medicare. One important item to note is that you are not automatically enrolled in Medicare. This can be a source of confusion at times, that once you reach age 65 you are enrolled into Medicare automatically. That is not so, you must make the election to enroll.

Are you eligible?

Like the Social Security eligibility requirements, if you have worked (or your spouse) and paid into Medicare taxes for 10

---

[20]http://kff.org/medicare/issue-brief/an-overview-of-medicare/
[21]http://www.forbes.com/forbes/welcome/?toURL=http://www.forbes.com/sites/dandiamond/2015/07/13/aging-in-america-10000-people-enroll-in-medicare-every-day

years then you are eligible for Medicare. Once you are age 65 you can enroll in Social Security benefits. If you are retired and no longer covered by an employer sponsored group health insurance plan, you should sign up as soon as eligible. If you are still working beyond 65 and covered by a group plan, it can be a little complicated, and we will address those questions in just a moment.

Medicare Basics:

First let's look at some of the way basics of Medicare, what is covered, what it costs, etc.

Original Medicare is Parts A and B of Medicare.

Here is what is covered by these parts:

Part A of Medicare:

Part A is coverage for:
- Hospital care
- Skilled nursing facility care
- Short-term nursing home care
- Home health care services
- Hospice

There is no out of pocket premium cost for Part A as long as you have the necessary years of covered earnings that paid Medicare tax.

Part B of Medicare:

Part B is coverage for many of the more daily needs:
- Doctor visits
- Lab tests
- Medical equipment
- Emergency room

The out of pocket premiums are based on income levels each year and are at these current levels: for a Joint Filer with income of $170,000 or less, the cost is $134.00 per month (in 2018).

With income above $170,000, the premiums will increase. The maximum cost for Medicare is $428.60 per month (in 2018). This cost is per individual that is covered by Medicare part B.

Part D of Medicare:

I know we just skipped over Part C, but we will get back to that in just a moment because it is a little complicated. Part D is the drug coverage option. It is not required, but is certainly recommended to assist with cost related to prescription drugs. The premium for Part D is primarily based on coverage and from which carrier you use for coverage. These plans can run anywhere from $10/month to over $100/month. One item to mention is that if your income is over certain levels ($170,000 joint income) then you will pay your plan premium plus an income based adjustment.

Medi-Gap Policies:

Like Employer based health insurance, Medicare has holes in it where you will have to come out of pocket for some services. The Medi-Gap policies are a way to lessen the potential out of pocket expenses. Medi-Gap policies all carry a monthly premium, with various services covered at various levels for different plans. A Medi-Gap policy may run $100 or more per month, but it may provide coverage for a number of items like travel outside the US that many may find helpful.

Part C:

Now we've come back to what Part C is of Medicare. Part C is for the Medicare Advantage policies. These policies are used for retiree health care needs just like Parts A and B of Original Medicare, but these policies typically provide more of an all in one solution, with coverage levels that may be on par with Medi-Gap policies.

Medicare Advantage policies are likened to HMO or PPO plans that you may be familiar with in regard to Employer based health insurance. These policies may provide a simpler all in one solution for one fixed cost, but one key item to consider is that by way of the HMO or PPO similarity, they may have restrictions on who you can use as a provider. You should ensure that your providers are in network to prevent surprises after you have signed up. As well, there could be issues if you are traveling (which is what retirees like to do!) and cannot find a provider in network if a need arises.

A Medicare Advantage plan can combine all coverages of Parts A, B, D and Medi-Gap policies into one. This is appealing to many folks for the simplicity and could make sense for you if you do not have concerns around the in-network and out-of-network complexity.

Annual Open Enrollment:

Every year between October 15th and December 7th is the annual open enrollment period for Medicare. If you went with one coverage the prior year, but would like to make elections to try something different, you can do so each year during the open enrollment period. Any changes will take effect beginning January 1st of the following year.

Making your decision:

The keys to making your Medicare decisions are general the following:

- Does your Medicare elections of parts A, B, D, and Medi-Gap or simply Medicare Advantage best meet your expected needs?
- If you prefer a Medicare Advantage plan do you have concerns about the convenience of being able to use in-network providers?
- From a cost standpoint, what makes the most sense for out of pocket premiums, coverage gaps that you will need to fund, and other out of pocket expenses?

Long-Term Care needs:

When it comes to Long-Term care, I'm always reminded of this story I heard one time.

"It's a bright early morning and your friend who is a banker gives you a call out of the blue. He sounds panicked and tells you that he isn't sure which bank is going under today, but he's gotten word that there is a bank that will go under, and if you don't take your money out, you will lose it when the bank closes. You only have time to go to one bank. He knows the three potential banks that may close and tells you that Bank A has a 1% of failing, Bank B has a 50% chance of failing and bank C has a 20% chance of failing. You think about the odds and realize that at these three banks you have the following in deposit at each one. Bank A you have $200,000, Bank B you have $300,000 and bank C you have $30,000."

The question becomes which bank you are going to? I'm sure you understand the illustration and have deduced that Bank B represents the potential chance of needing Long-Term Care later in life. These figures are pulled from a Genworth study that indicates the potential chance of having a total loss of home by fire is about a 1% chance, this is represented by the $200,000 figure. There is about a 20% chance of having a wreck and totaling your vehicle, this is represented by the $30,000 figure. Lastly, for someone attaining age 65, there is a 50% chance of having a long-term care need. This is a need that is a lasting and significantly expensive need.

Recent figures suggest the cost of a nursing home is around $80,000 — $90,000 per year. The average stay is estimated to last around 3 years, therefore imputing a total cost if a care arises of around $250,000 — $300,000 per individual.

Understanding Long-Term Care:

Basics:

Long-term care is used to pay for care that is expected to

last and requires ongoing care. To qualify as a long-term care event and for the coverage to begin, you typically should not be able to do at least two Activities of Daily Living (ADL's).

Here is a standard list of ADL's:
- Transferring yourself from one place to another
- Bathing and Showering
- Dressing
- Self-Feeding
- Personal hygiene and grooming
- Going to the bathroom

What does it cover?

Long-term care can cover assistance for the care of oneself in a variety of ways. Some benefits of a policy can be used to provide Home Health care services, assisted living, and lastly complete ongoing care at a nursing home facility.

A policy can provide coverage that will kick in for any of these needs and for in any of these types of environments.

How to pay for it?

There are only a few ways to pay for long-term care needs:
1. Self-pay
2. Medicare – which is extremely limited to 20 days of care for skilled care and then 80 additional days with a high out of pocket cost to the retiree.
3. Medi-caid – which only begins if all other financial assets have been completely exhausted (for the most part) for someone.

4. Long-Term care insurance - this is potentially the most appropriate option to protect against severe financial issues that can abound with the other options above.

How do I get Long-Term care insurance?

Long-Term care insurance is available through many different carriers. Each policy is different and will have different coverage levels. Most will provide a specific amount of coverage per day and a lifetime maximum of benefits paid. Many will have Cost of Living Adjustment (COLA) options to attempt to keep pace with increasing cost of care over the long term. The premiums can be paid a number of ways, from a onetime payment to payments over a lifetime.

Hybrid Policies:

Over the past number of years, hybrid policies have become more popular. These types of policies are created on a life insurance or annuity type framework and will carry a rider (an option) to cover long-term care needs. These policies can allow someone to have a multiple use policy that may cover them with life insurance that provides cash value, a death benefit, or dollars to be used for Long-term care needs.

These can make sense for some people that are worried about paying into a long-term care policy for a lifetime, and if they die without having a care need, all the premiums were paid for nothing of value. These hybrid policies allow a potential policy owner to use the policy for Long-term care needs if a need arises, to receive some of their premiums paid in back by way of cash value or if they pass without using care, a death benefit will pass to their heirs.

One way to fund these types of policies is through a tax-free 1035 exchange. If you have an old cash value whole life insurance policy with cash surrender value, this can be used to fund the premium cost of a hybrid LTC policy.

There are certainly many decisions to make when it comes to Long-term care needs. The best plan is simply to have a plan in place. Every situation is unique and it will make sense for some to self-insure while it will make sense for others to plan on using a long-term care policy to meet their needs.

Life insurance:

For retirees, typically their need for life insurance diminishes once retirement begins. The core use of life insurance is typically to provide for the financial needs of a surviving spouse or family if the income earning power is lost by a deceased spouse or parent.

Since a retiree has already stopped working, they are planning on using their saved assets to live off of and life insurance may not be too important from a pure financial standpoint. There could be a number of reasons to continue carrying life insurance, and I will address a few here:

Term vs. Whole Life:

Term life insurance covers a specific person for a specific period of time. These policies can last 5 years to 30 years. Many people will set up a term policy that will last until age 65 (or their expected retirement age). Since they would retire and expect to be financially independent at that time, from a financial standpoint, this strategy can make a lot of sense.

Term policies are fairly inexpensive and provide a specific premium cost for the specific period of time. They are simple and easy to understand.

A whole life insurance policy is a policy that is used to provide a life insurance need for life. The premiums can be paid out of pocket for the entire life of the policy or until there is enough cash value in the policy to strategically pay for the premiums internally.

These types of policies also create a cash surrender value that can be used as a financial asset or used to provide a loan to yourself from the policy. Over a long period of time, the internal rate of return may provide an inflation plus a little extra type return.

If you have one of these policies and have owned it for over thirty years, it may not be too bad from an investment standpoint, but a whole life policy should never be confused from the onset of purchasing as an investment; it is an insurance policy that over a real long period of time can provide something similar to an investment return (a pretty safe investment).

Because of the dual purpose of whole life insurance and the lifetime coverage it certainly carries a much higher monthly expense than term coverage. Be mindful of this when purchasing a policy.

Taxability of life insurance proceeds:

Life insurance proceeds are received tax free. If a loved one dies and you are the beneficiary, the death benefit is paid to you without tax.

The death benefit is included in the taxable estate of the one that passed. Be mindful of this as it can cause someone to have a much larger taxable estate than they thought.

There are several decisions to make when reviewing life insurance coverage. We've only covered the basics and every person's situation is unique.

6

THE RETIREMENT ESTATE PLAN

Are you planning for the known unknown of death and transference of assets?

This is the 2018 update of Retirement Planning Blueprint® and it comes with good news from an estate tax standpoint. The Tax Cut and Jobs Act that was signed into law on December 22, 2018 has increased the Federal estate exemption levels. Based on this new law, the Federal estate exemption levels allow for one person in 2018 to die with an estate worth up to $11,200,000 dollars before having estate tax issues. A couple could die with a total estate value of $22,400,000 without estate tax due.

If the likelihood of owing estate tax is so low for so many people, then the question becomes: why even work on estate planning?

There are a number of reasons why estate planning is still extremely important.

Estate Planning Basics:

Estate planning is the process of coordinating how you would like your estate wishes to be carried out at death. Estate Planning often refers to establishing how you would like your health care and financial needs to be administered in the event of incapacity.

By going through the estate planning process prior to incapacity or death you are able to determine how your estate assets will be distributed, define what your wishes are for your estate and who will carry them out. If you still have minor children, this process is extremely important, because you will also define who will serve as custodians for your children.

Basic Estate Planning Documents:

There are a few common core documents for an estate plan. These are the typical documents that an attorney will likely set up if you go want to set up your documents for an estate plan.

The common core four would be:

1. Last Will & Testament
2. Health Care Power of Attorney
3. Living Will
4. Durable Financial Power of Attorney

The following will serve as a brief description of each of these core documents:

Last Will & Testament:

This is perhaps the document most folks are familiar with. This documents how you would like any assets that will pass through your will to flow (we will discuss later that some assets do not pass through your will). In your will, you will state how you want assets to be distributed and to whom. You will also appoint some key people in your will. You will state who will serve as your Executor, who is the person that will carry out the wishes of your will. If a trust is funded through your will, you will also state who will serve as the Trustee of the trusts in your will. If you have minor children, you will establish who the Guardian of the children will be for them.

Each of these roles are vitally important to ensure that your wishes are carried out properly. Often you will state a primary person for these roles as well as an alternate or two if that person is unable or chooses not to serve.

One important word to note here is the term probate. Probate is the process of proving the will. In the probate process, the executor of an estate would go through the probate court to carry out the wishes of the will. This process requires time and expense for the executor and the estate.

Health Care Power of Attorney:

Your Health Care Power of Attorney will be in charge of making medical decisions on your behalf if you are incapacitated. The person you elect for this role should be someone you feel comfortable and confident with making these decisions for you. It is important to discuss what you would want them to do in various health care situations during the planning process. You will typically elect a primary agent and then one or two secondary agents, if the primary is unable or chooses not to serve.

Living will (advanced directive):

The living will places on file your wishes before a life threatening medical event occurs. You will state during the planning process various decisions around artificial nutrition and other decisions that could prolong life. You will need to work with an attorney to understand how the living will and health care power of attorney work together, as this can be complex and state specific.

Durable Financial Power of Attorney:

The financial power of attorney will perform any functions regarding the management of your finances if you are incapacitated. They will be able to handle your financial accounts and obligations on your behalf at this time. It is important to ensure that you have someone that you are confident and comfortable with to take on this role for you. You will want to work with them during the planning process to ensure they understand their role and responsibility.

Advanced Estate Planning Document:

You may have heard about the Revocable Living Trust (RLT) document. The RLT is a slightly more advanced document and not one that is necessary for everyone to put into place. There are some misconceptions of what a RLT is used for. Let me first state what it is not used for. It is not a planning document to avoid or lower income taxes or estate taxes. A RLT does nothing in the way of saving taxes.

There are two primary reasons to use a RLT. The first reason is to avoid probate on assets that would normally pass through your will and therefore be subject to probate. This will save probate costs, time for the executor of the estate, and provide a smoother transition of property from the estate to beneficiaries. The second reason a RLT is useful is to keep the estate of a decedent private. A probated will is a public document and is not provided privacy from claims of creditors or peeking eyes of the public. A RLT can be used to keep the details of the estate private and out of the public eye. This is how when famous and well known people pass away details about their estate and disposition of assets become well known.

Other important Estate Planning items:

There are a few other items that are important to know and understand with your estate planning. One of the most important items to note is that some accounts will not pass through your will.

Beneficiary designations:

These accounts are anything that have beneficiaries designated. These would be accounts like your Employer Sponsored Retirement Accounts, Individual Retirement Accounts (IRA's), Roth IRA's, Annuities, or Life insurance. All of these type accounts require the account owner to place beneficiaries on file. At the death of the account owner, the beneficiary would simply submit a death certificate, and the account will pass to the beneficiary without going through the probate process. It is very important to understand that your beneficiaries on file will trump the last will and testament directions. For instance if you are divorced and still have your ex-spouse on file as your beneficiary of your IRA account, but you have your children listed in your will, the IRA will pass to your ex-spouse at your death if it is not corrected.

Payable or Transfer on Death (POD/TOD):

Many accounts, such as your checking accounts, after-tax investment accounts, or other liquid investment accounts that do not require beneficiary designations, will go by way of your will and through the probate process. There is a way to avoid this and that is by placing the equivalent of a beneficiary on file by using POD/TOD designations onto these accounts. By doing so, you will accomplish the same benefit that beneficiaries on file of retirements accounts provide, which is a quick and easy passing of assets to your heirs.

Key figures for your Estate Planning:

As we reviewed earlier, there are a few key figures for estate planning purposes. One of those figures is the max estate size that a person can have before federal estate tax is due. This is currently in 2018 at $11,200,000 per person or $22,400,000 per couple. This is a sizable figure and one that most folks are likely to never attain. If you are in the place where you are over these levels there is some planning that you can look at to lower yourself below the thresholds.

It is also important to note that some states may still have an estate tax on the state level. Some states are unified with the Federal levels, while others are independent of the state levels and carry their own max estate levels before state estate tax is due.

One strategy is annual gifting to kids, grandkids, friends, and other family. You can provide a gift of $14,000 per year to any person without a gift tax penalty (current amount for 2018). This strategy can be helpful to begin lowering your estate levels and provide you with the benefit of seeing some of your heirs use assets that would pass to them at your death.

There are a couple other strategies with trusts that can be used to remove assets from your estate that can lower your estate below the max exemption levels. As well, any assets that are given to charity at your death are not included in your taxable estate and can provide a way to prevent estate tax from being paid on levels that are above the max estate levels.

Two important Estate Planning ideas:

There two last estate planning ideas that I would like to mention. One is a planning strategy that could prevent sizable taxes from being paid, and the second is a planning point to

ensure the disposition of assets that pass by the beneficiary
are properly dispersed.

Step up in basis:

In the current tax code, assets inherited are provided what
is called a step up in basis. This is important to understand
because often times parents or grandparents (or perhaps you)
have assets that have significant appreciation. These are often
assets that have been held for a long time and have gone up
in value over that long period of time. This could be a stock
position that was purchased 50 years ago, an old family farm
or property, or a number of other items that would have an
original purchase price and a current fair market value.

With the step up in basis provision a beneficiary that inherits
an appreciated asset will take over the basis on the date
of death as their basis, instead of taking a carryover basis
amount, which would be the basis that the original owner had
at purchase. For example, if someone owned a large amount
of stock that totaled $100,000 and was purchased for $10,000
50 years ago, the step up in basis provision would allow the
beneficiary to now have a basis in the stock of $100,000. This
would allow the $90,000 of embedded capital gains to be
escaped without tax being owed. If the original owner basis
was carried over to the beneficiary, then capital gains would
be owed on the $90,000 (if the beneficiary sold the stock).

Understand the Per Stirpes Designation:

Lastly, I would like to point out one little box that typically
appears on beneficiary designation forms. It is a box that is
listed on the form beside the designation of a beneficiary and

states "Per stirpes". The per stirpes designation will cause an account to be split in equal shares among the children of a beneficiary if the beneficiary on file pre-deceases the account owner. Why is this important you may ask, here is an example of what this could look like.

Dad and mom are married and die simultaneously in an accident. The beneficiaries on file are their two sons. One of the two sons has two children. The other son does not have any children. If the son with children also dies with dad and mom and the per stirpes election was not taken on the beneficiary form, then the account will pass fully to the surviving son, and the grandchildren (children of the beneficiary) are not entitled to any part of the account. The account has passed per capita, or in other words, by generation. Since there was only one surviving beneficiary in that generation they will receive the account in full. This is a very important element of estate planning because most people have significant assets held in accounts that will pass by beneficiary. It is important to verify with your investment custodians that hold your accounts that will pass by beneficiary how exactly your accounts would pass if a situation like that described above were to take place. You will want to ensure that the accounts would pass in line with your wishes.

When to review your Estate Plan:

There are a number of times and events it would be important to review your estate plan. You want to ensure that your current planning aligns with your current wishes. Here are times that it would be recommended to review your estate plan:

1. If death occurs of someone that is listed in your will.

2. If you go through a divorce or remarriage.

3. If your spouse dies.

4. If you give birth to a new child, or if you have a new grandchild.

5. If your minor children become of age.

6. If you have a significant change in your personal financial situation.

7. If you move to a different state.

8. If new estate laws come into effect.

9. If you desire to change key roles in your estate plan (such as your executor, trustee, beneficiary, power of attorneys, etc.).

As you can see, even with estate exemption levels at such high levels, there is still an abundance of planning to do with your estate plan. The key is to set up your estate plan before death or incapacity to ensure that all your wishes will be carried out as simply and effectively as possible.

Wrapping it up:

As you can see, there is a lot that goes into building a comprehensive retirement plan. The key to remember is that the benefits of having peace in retirement will far outweigh the stress of having to take time to understand it all on the front end. Spend time to understand your building blocks, the tools, and techniques available to provide you with a long-term retirement plan. This is what the Retirement Planning Blueprint® is all about. Helping you have peace of mind as you enter and live in retirement.

7

Putting everything together:

To pull all of this together, I want to lay out a sample Case Study that will provide context of how a comprehensive plan would work together:

Case Facts:

- Jack and Jill, both age 64 want to retire at age 66.
- Jack earns $100,000 from a local company.
- Jill works part-time and earns $20,000.
- Jack's Social Security benefit at 66 (FRA) is estimated to be $2,600.
- Jill's Social Security benefit at 66 (FRA) is estimated to be $1,000.
- Between IRA's and 401k's, Jack's assets total $600,000.
- Between IRA's and 401k's, Jill's assets total $150,000.
- They have a joint investment account with assets of $150,000.
- They have cash in the amount of $100,000.
- They just made the last payment on their mortgage.
- They would like to spend $5,000 per month in retirement, as well as $10,000/year on Family experiences. Creates an Income Gap of around $2,300/month after accounting for Social Security benefits. Inflation on expenses of 3%/year.
- They currently have 70% in stock mutual funds and 30% in bond mutual funds. There is no clear income strategy to meet the income gap.

What they want to know:

Retirement Plan:

- Do they have enough to retire and spend as they desire?
- Will their assets last beyond normal life expectancy?

Income Plan:

- How much do they need from their portfolio each year?

- Will they be able to make up the income gap with their current investment strategy?

Tax Plan:
- They have low basis stock that they want to diversify?
- They want to keep taxes minimal until Required Distributions begin, but also want to pay any taxes that make sense if they can at lower rates today.

Investment Plan:
- Are the funds allocated in a way that will mitigate risk in a 2008 type draw drown?
- What allocation should they have to stock / bonds?

Risk Management Plan:
- They prefer to pay extra premiums for Medicare options to ensure.
- They would like LTC coverage, but are hesitant to pay too much out of pocket for premium expense.

Estate Plan:
- They have not updated their estate document in many years.
- They want to review everything, so that probate can be avoided and everything passes smoothly.

Solutions to consider and implement:

Retirement Plan:
- A review of their Retirement Plan and Monte Carlo Analysis indicates their plan is set up for success, even with a very conservative rate of return.

Income Plan:

- We recommend that a bond ladder be set up to meet income needs with defined interest and principal maturities to meet cash flow needs.
- Bond ladder will be replenished if stocks are high and will continue to be drawn down if stocks are down, until they recover.
- We recommend they elect a restricted application for Jack of Jill's benefits, so that Jack's can continue to grow until age 70 and provide maximum survivor benefits if he pre-deceases Jill.

Tax Plan:

- In the first tax year after retirement, we recommend to live off of bond interest and maturities through the taxable investment account.
- By doing so, they are able to sell the low basis capital gain stock in full ($50,000 of capital gains) and not pay capital gains taxes since they are under the taxable income limits for 0% capital gains rates.
- After the first year, they will live off of the remaining taxable investment account and some cash (although they would like to not go lower than $30,000 in cash).
- This will allow a small amount to be pulled forward by way of Roth conversion in the 12% bracket vs. the 24% bracket as they would if they did nothing, but have RMD's due at age 70.5.
- Net Unrealized Appreciation was also elected on $10,000 of basis of stock to allow for long-term capital gains treatment in a future year vs. ordinary income.

Investment Plan:

- Their current allocation is 70% in stocks and 30% in bonds. In a 50% market decline (2008, 2000 – 2002 type events), the account would likely experience a 30%+ decline.
- They did not realize this much risk was in their portfolio.
- There was no clear strategy to meet income needs.
- To better structure their portfolio to lower risk and meet income needs, they moved the next 10 years of withdrawals into an individual bond defined maturity ladder.
- Due to the lower social security benefits between ages 65 – 70, the total amount moved over was $500,000. This includes approximately a 15% buffer for unexpected needs.
- This positions their portfolio around a 50/50 allocation and provides a defined strategy to meet income needs.

Risk Management Plan:

- Since they prefer to have less risk associated with out of pocket expenses in retirement, they will sign up for Medicare with a Medi-Gap supplemental policy.
- They could achieve similar results with a Medicare Advantage plan, but their doctors are accessible with the Medicare option.
- They want to insure against Long-Term Care but do not want to "throw away" premiums. They elect for a hybrid policy on each individual that allows for a return of premium, death benefit or benefit coverage.
- They also had an old Whole Life insurance policy with

$80,000 of cash value that was converted into this hybrid option for Jack with no other premiums out of pocket.

Estate Planning:

- They reviewed their old wills and noted that the current executor was Jack's brother. They preferred to change this to their oldest son.
- Their beneficiary designations were properly on file.
- To avoid probate in the event of simultaneous death, they added their three children in thirds as Transfer on Death to their Joint brokerage account and checking accounts.
- They are contemplating the use of a Revocable Living Trust, but realize their home and cars may be the only items that would pass by way of the will.

As you can see, there are a number of strategic planning opportunities to think through as you create your Retirement Planning Blueprint®. Your retirement plan is like a number of puzzle pieces that all work together to create a plan that is unique to you. These pieces when positioned properly will create clarity and confidence for you as you enter retirement and beyond.

8

DO YOU NEED A GUIDE?

Should you work with an advisor or go it alone?

After learning about everything that goes into building your Retirement Planning Blueprint® the real question becomes: do you do it yourself, or do you work with an advisor to serve as your long-term retirement planning guide?

After working with clients for over 10 years, I've come to realize that many fear working with an advisor because there are several unknowns that must be dealt with. I wanted to provide some thoughts on what it looks like to work with an advisor.

Financial Advisor 101:

Let's start from the top and figure out what a Financial Advisor even is and does.

What do you do?

This is always a funny question to ask a Financial Advisor. In advisor sales roles, we are even taught to answer this a certain way to evoke more questions from the person asking. It can become pretty odd, to be honest with you.

The reason this tends to happen is due to the ambiguity of being a Financial Advisor. Unlike being a lawyer or doctor, there isn't a clear requirement to pass to become a Financial Advisor. There are various licensing tests that can be taken to provide some credence, but even some of those do very little to create true competence criteria to evaluate advisors.

Instead of Financial Advisor, you may also hear, Financial Planner, Retirement Planner, Wealth Manager, Income Planner, Wealth Advisor, Retirement Advisor, Income Advisor, Private Wealth Advisor. I'm sure there are more beyond this as well.

I believe the two best ways (without knowing anything else about the advisor) to assess competence and confidence is to know if they work comprehensively and if they work on the same side of the table as their clients.

Working comprehensively – Why does it matter?

As you've seen throughout this book, there is a lot more to think about when it comes to your retirement planning than simply life insurance, an annuity, or just your investments. There are many decisions to make around taxes, risk management, and income planning.

I believe, the most appropriate planning considers each of these areas. To determine quickly a general competence by the advisor in these areas is to see if he/she is a Certified Financial Planner™. By obtaining a CFP® you can be assured they have a baseline understanding of each of these areas and should be able to help you align your planning decisions in an optimal way.

Advisor Alphabet Soup:

It can also be helpful to understand the Alphabet Soup of Advisor initials. There are many that someone can achieve and place on a business card. I will steer you to look for what I will call the top 3:

1. CFP® - Certified Financial Planner™
2. CFA – Chartered Financial Analyst
3. CPA – Certified Public Accountant

These three require hundreds of study hours and multi-hour or section exams. Many others can be obtained rather quickly and will require much less time, work, and understanding to obtain.

What are your fees?

A reasonable question, but one people fail to understand and to ask is to inquire of all the fees a client will be paying. We often hear of the advisor fee, but other important fees such as expense ratios, money manager fees, and trade fees may be swept under the proverbial rug.

Here is some information you should know when it comes to fees.

- Most ongoing advisor relationships will require an investment management fee. This fee is often around 1% of the total amount that you invest with the advisor. If you have $500,000 with the advisor, the annual advisor fee would be $5,000 per year. Typically, this fee is deducted on a quarterly basis, so ¼ of $5,000 would be $1,250 each quarter.
- You may be able to find an advisor that will set this fee up as on ongoing flat fee retainer. For instance, you and the advisor may agree to a quarterly fee of $1,000 per quarter. That would simply be the fee, and no calculation would be used or required on a quarterly basis.

Another important fee to know is the expense ratios and any money manager fees that you may pay as well:

- Expense ratios for active mutual funds could be at a level of 1.0% or higher and passive funds are likely 50% or lower.
- If an advisor uses an outside money manager or subadvisor, you need to be aware of that fee as well.

The reasons fees matter is this example: If you have an advisor fee of 1.5% and a portfolio full of active mutual funds with an average expense ratio of 1.0%, then you must overcome 2.5% of fees just to begin making money. Likewise, if you have an advisor that charges .75% and portfolio expenses of .30%, then you must overcome 1.05% before making money. This could make a considerable difference over a life-time of investing.

Fiduciary – Acting in your best interest:

The term fiduciary is at the forefront of much discussion in the Financial Advisor industry. It is ideal to find an Advisor that is a Fiduciary to ensure that their advice aligns with your needs. It may be difficult to believe there are advisors that would not align advice with their client's best interest, but they are certainly alive and well.

The key is to ensure that they adhere to the Fiduciary standard of care and will only make recommendations that are in the best interest of their client. This is very important, and one requirement that I would recommend you have when identifying an advisor to work with.

How to find the best advisor for you?

There are thousands of advisors. How would you ever find one that is appropriate for you?

I would recommend understanding these four key areas when interviewing an advisor:

1. **Advice** – Do they provide comprehensive advice or simply specific to one area?

2. **Service** – Do they have service standards of how you will work together? Will they work for you on an ongoing basis?

3. **Relationship** – You need to enjoy working with this person, do you? Do you trust them and feel confident in their advice for you?

4. **Cost** – Are their costs in line with other options? You should ensure their total costs are not too high, compared to the averages and others that could serve you.

As you can see, there are number of factors to consider when you think about working with an advisor. I work with many clients and know many other advisors. The best client relationships are the ones that we envision working with for decades to come. This is important to recognize on the front end to ensure that you select an advisor that you can work with for all the years of retirement.

APPENDIX

Recap of Session one of Retirement Planning Blueprint®:

Six Plans for Retirement

- Retirement Plan
- Tax Plan
- Income Plan
- Investment Plan
- Risk Management Plan
- Estate Plan

Retirement Plan:

- Two big questions:
  - o Do I have enough to retire?
  - o Do I have a plan to not outlive my money?
- Define "What does retirement mean for me"?
  - o What will you spend your time doing?

- o If you have planned and understand your plan excess, how would you allocate among the three choices that you have:
  - Increase Family Experiences
  - Increase Family Legacy
  - Increase Charitable Legacy
- Create your one-page retirement plan:
- o Income & Expenses
  - Defined income in retirement
  - Defined expense in retirement
  - The difference between the Defined income and Defined expense will be your Income Gap
  - Does your Annual Income Gap exceed 4% annual withdrawals from your liquid assets?
  - If your withdrawal rate is around 4%, your plan, based on historical measures, has a strong chance of success.
  - If your withdrawal rate is higher than 5%, then without specific changes, it may be difficult to sustain a 30 year retirement period. You have a few options to close the gap:
    - Work longer
    - Make more prior to planned retirement
    - Spend less before, after or during retirement

- o Assets & Liabilities
  - What are your liquid assets?
    - Checking account
    - Savings account
    - 401k/403b
    - IRA
    - Roth IRA
    - Total Liquid Assets
  - What are your non-liquid assets?
    - Personal residence equity
    - Rental real estate
    - Business equity
  - What are your liabilities
    - Mortgage
    - Auto loans

Tax Plan:

- Identify Tax Planning opportunities
  o Basic Planning
  o Advanced Planning
  o Planning before retirement
  o Planning after retirement

Income Plan:

- Social Security
  o Ensure you have accurate information regarding your social security benefits (www.ssa.gov) to set up an account

o Identify how you will take your social security benefits

o Identify how to coordinate with your spouse's benefits to maximize long-term benefits and survivor benefits

- Required Minimum Distributions
  o When will they begin?
  o How will this distribution affect your tax planning?

Recap of Session two of Retirement Planning Blueprint®:

Investment Plan:

- Understand your Investment mix.
- Understand the risk in your portfolio.
- Understand how your time horizon affects your investment allocation.
- Understand your risk tolerance and historical risk/return of your current investment mix.
- Define your ideal investment strategy to meet your remaining income gap:
  o Total Return approach
  o Income Floor approach
  o Defined Income approach
- Ensure that you clearly have a plan in place to

mitigate the risk associated with Sequence of Returns risk.

Risk Management Plan:

- Review Medicare basics:
  o Original Medicare
    - Part A - Hospital
    - Part B - Routine
  o Part D – Prescription drugs
  o Medicare Advantage
  o Medi-gap supplemental policies
- Identify preferred Medicare coverage:
  o Original Medicare or
  o Medicare Advantage
- Review Long-Term Care basics:
  o Average cost of care
  o Options to prepare for this potential expense
- Identify preferred way to cover cost of care

Estate Planning:

- Do you have the core four documents for your estate plan in place?
  o Last Will & Testament
  o Health Care Power of Attorney

o Financial Power of Attorney

o Living Will

- When was the last time your documents were updated?
- Do your documents properly outline the key people for your estate plan?

o Beneficiaries and breakdown of inheritance amounts

o Executor

o Trustee

o Guardians (if still minor children)

- Have you reviewed your beneficiary designations to ensure they align with the wishes of your estate plan?
- Review options for bank accounts or investment accounts (non-retirement) to ensure they transfer efficiently:

o Joint titling

o Payable on Death account titling

- If you have assets that will pass outside of beneficiary designations or account titling, should you consider a Revocable Living Trust as a part of your estate plan?
- Educate children or beneficiaries on deferring inherited accounts and not taking a lump sum:

o Lower their taxes vs. a one-time lump sum

o Provides for a "stretch IRA" that will only require minimum distributions annually based on their life expectancies

- Ensure if you desire for grandchildren to receive parent's inheritance portion (if they pre-decrease), that you make sure your desires are clearly indicated and per stirpes is elected on beneficiary designation.

Note pages for Retirement Planning Blueprint® class:

_____

_____

_____

_____

_____

_____

_____

_____

_____

_____

_____

_____

_____

_____

_____

_____

_____

_____

_____

_____

_____

_____

_____

_____

_____

_____

_____

_____

_____

_____

_____

_____

_____

_____

_____

_____

_____

_____

_____

_____

_____

_____

_____

_____

_____

_____

_____

_____

_____

_____

_____

_____

_____

_____

_____

_____

Made in the USA
Columbia, SC
30 December 2018